The rocks and rivers of British Columbia

Walter Moberly

BOW RIVER, IN THE CANADIAN ROCKY MOUNTAINS.

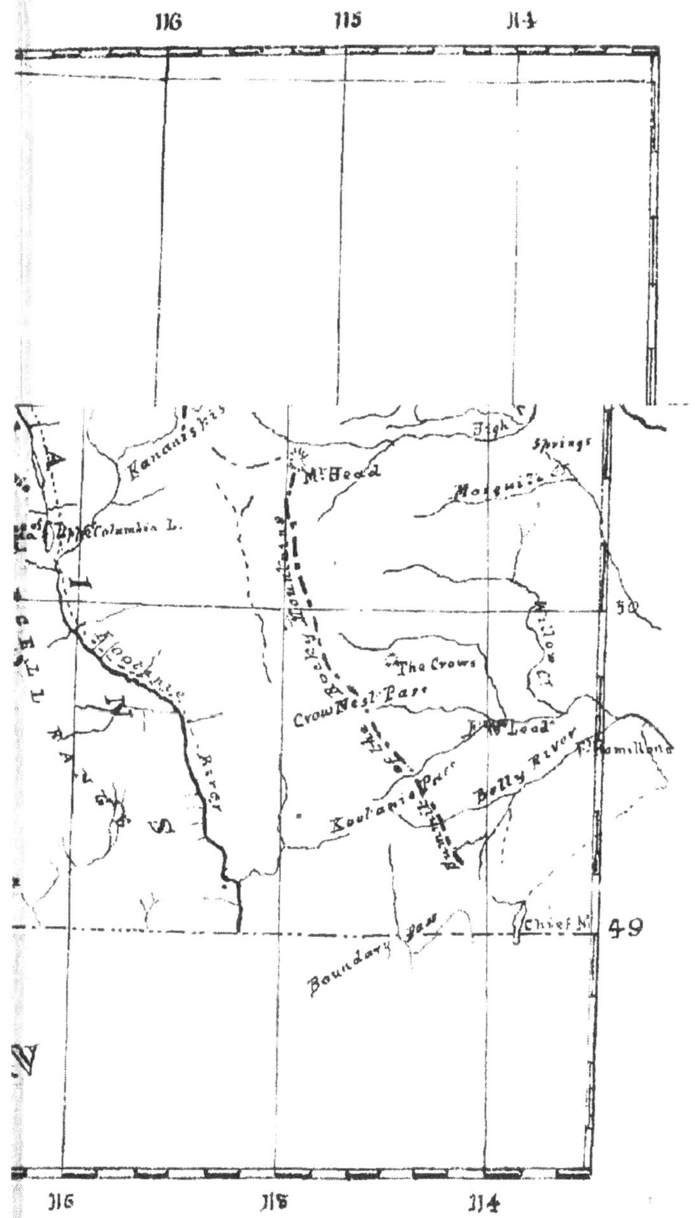
116
115
114
Kananaskis
Mt Head
Upper Columbia L.
Mosquito Cr.
Springs
50
Rocky Mountains
Kootanie
River
The Crows
Crow Nest Pass
Ft McLeod
Belly River
Kootanie Pass
Chief Mt
49
Boundary Pass
116
115
114

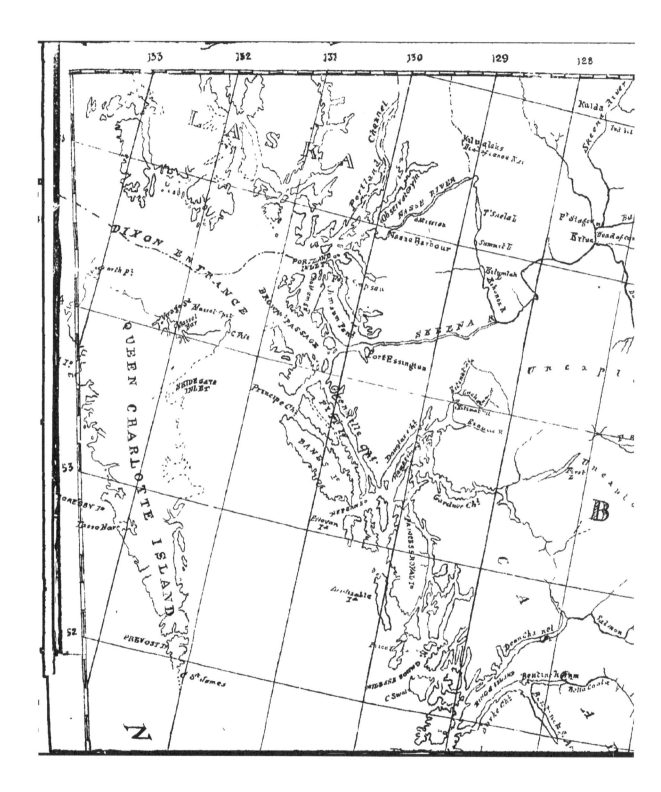

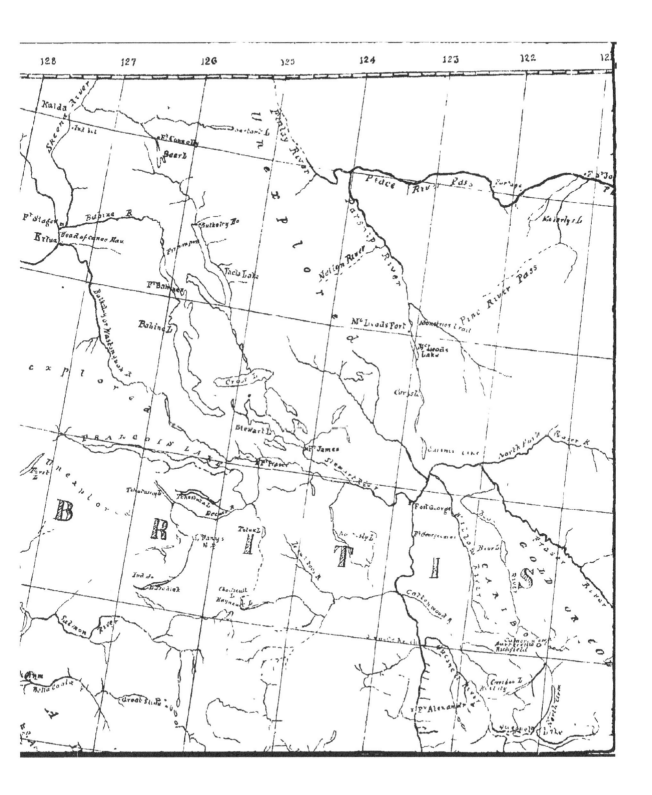

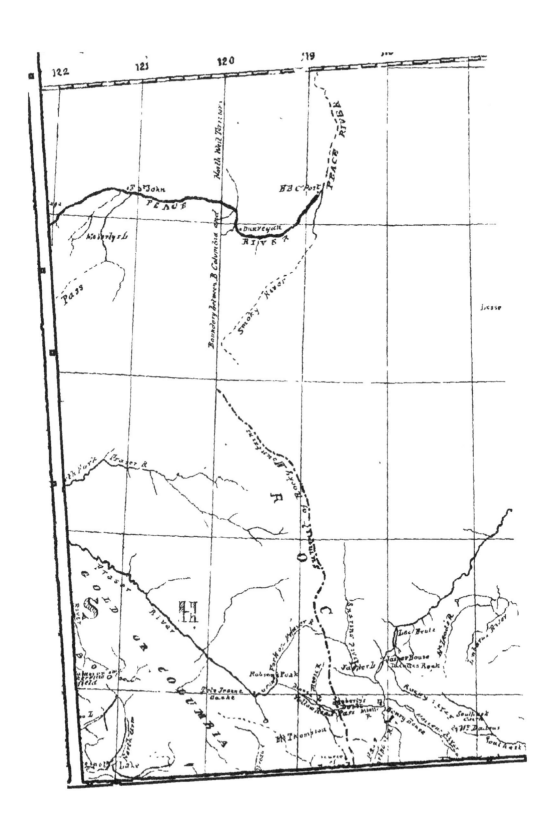

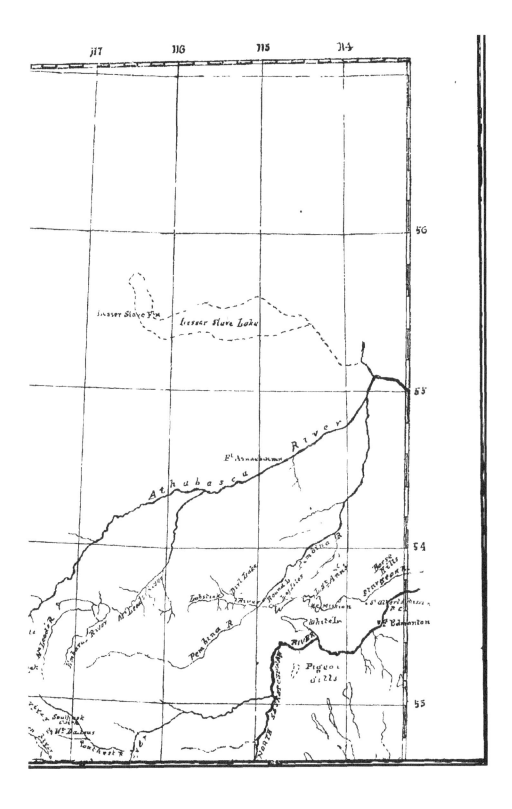

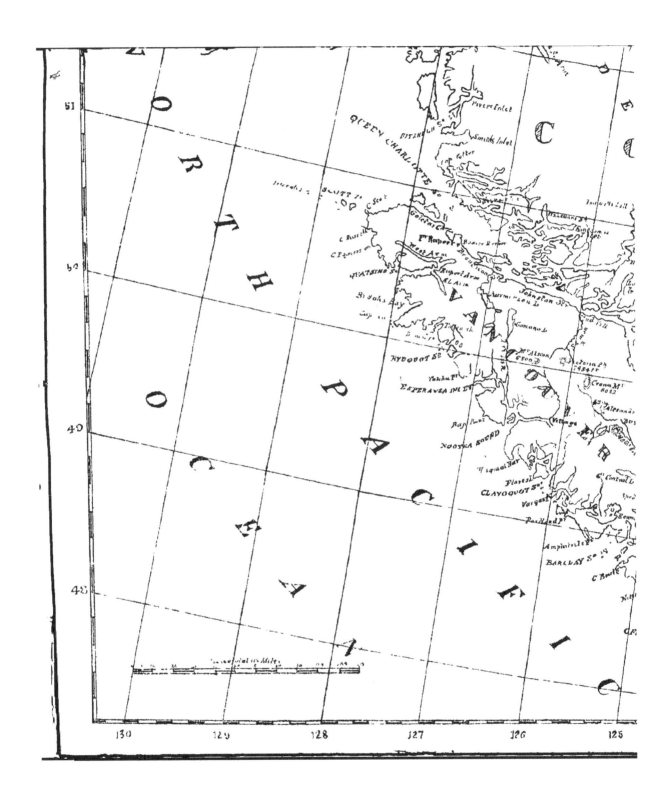

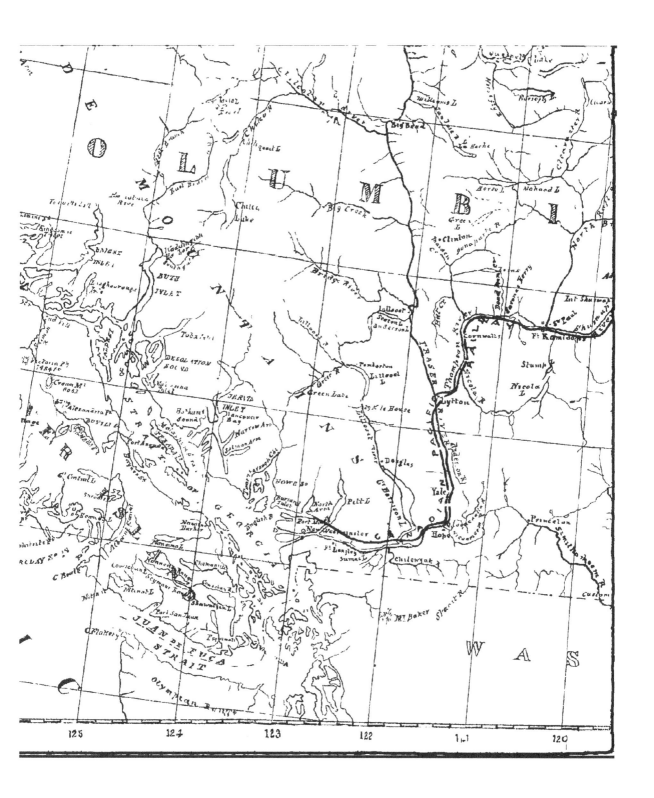

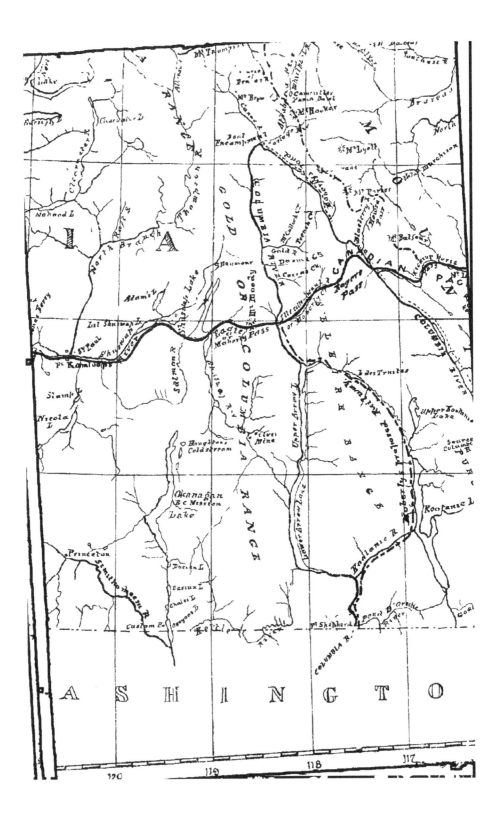

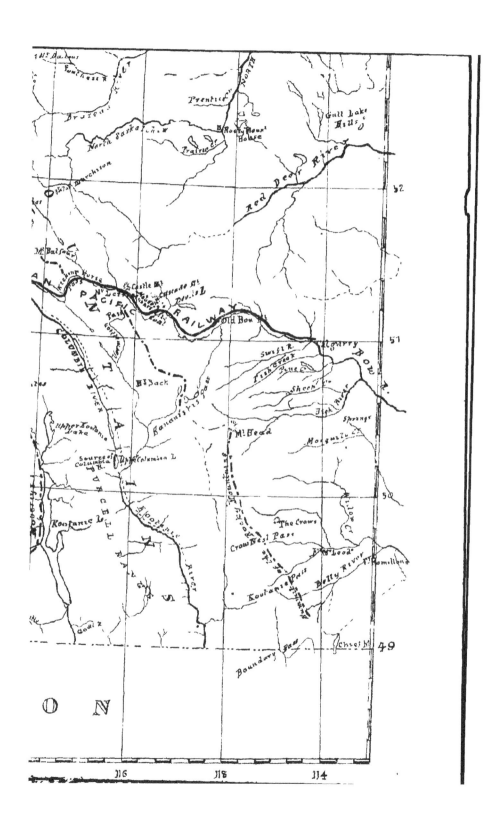

THE

B.

W A]

Late Assista

ment Engi

District of

P E

THE ROCKS AND RIVERS

OF

BRITISH COLUMBIA,

BY

WALTER MOBERLY, C.E.,

Late Assistant Surveyor-General of British Columbia and Dominion Govern-
ment Engineer-in-Charge of "Exploratory Surveys" of the Rocky Mountain
District of the "Canadian Pacific Railway."

London:
PRINTED BY H. BLACKLOCK & CO.,
75, FARRINGDON ROAD.

1885.

T HE

T e

gigantic

nation

the imp

in the (

in part

was a (

Dominio

extent,]

by, and

Columbi

to you.

To M

DEDICATION.

———:0:———

THE gradual development of the Dominion of Canada by a comparatively small and scattered population, and the gigantic work undertaken by them to consolidate and build up a nation worthy of the grand old British Empire, together with the important geographical position British Columbia occupies in the Confederation, has led me to write a few pages describing in part some of the events that occurred when British Columbia was a Crown Colony, and more recently a portion of the Dominion of Canada, and with both of which I was, to some extent, personally acquainted. The warm interest always taken by, and my early acquaintance with, you when in British Columbia induces me to dedicate my small and imperfect work to you.

WALTER MOBERLY,

WINNIPEG, *September*, 1884.

To MAJOR-GENERAL RICHARD CLEMENT MOODY,
Royal Engineers.

INDEX.

—o—

THE

ROCKS AND RIVERS OF BRITISH COLUMBIA.

CHAPTER I.

In the year 1854 I had the pleasure of forming a very intimate acquaintance with the celebrated Canadian painter, Mr. Paul Kane, of Toronto, after his journey across the mountains and visit to the Pacific Coast: and during that and the succeeding years, up to 1858, I was almost daily in his studio or house. Mr. Kane gave me long and most minute descriptions of the various places he had visited, and shewed me all his sketches, paintings, &c., &c., which he had collected.

His descriptions of the country interested me very much, and I decided to go there and see the Western or Pacific Coast, and try if such a thing as an overland communication could not be accomplished. Mr. Kane was on intimate terms with Sir George Simpson, Governor of the Hudson Bay Company, and I asked him to introduce me to Sir George, which he did. In my interview with Sir George I fully explained to him my wish to see Vancouver Island and British Columbia, and the ultimate object I had in view. Sir George at once most kindly offered me a letter of introduction to Mr., afterwards Sir James Douglas, at that time the head of the Honourable Hudson Bay Company on the Pacific Coast, and afterwards the first Governor of the Crown Colony of British Columbia. About this time I heard of gold having been discovered in British Columbia, and one fine morning, with Sir George Simpson's letter in my pocket, I started

for New York, to catch the steamer for the Isthmus of
Panama. On my reaching New York, I ascertained the first
steamer for the Isthmus would be the *Moses Taylor*, at that
time generally known as *The Rolling Moses*, and that I could
get the top bunk in a miserable state-room—only five tier of
bunks—by paying the full fare of 375 dollars, through to San
Francisco Money was scarce with me, and I walked up to the
St. Nicholas Hotel, where I was staying, in anything but a happy
state of mind I lit a cigar and considered the situation, and at
last concluded to go to St. Louis and join an emigrant train and
go overland by Salt Lake City With this intention I went to
call upon a friend, and told him the position I was in. His
answer was, " I have the very thing for you, come along " We
went down to a steamboat office and found a new company was
going to send the old steamer *Hermann*, round the Horn, to
Vancouver Island, in a few days, and that she would touch at Rio
Janeiro and other ports in South America, on her way. This
was very encouraging, as I should have the opportunity of seeing
something of South America, and of enjoying a pleasant passage
I accordingly engaged a very comfortable state-room, and saw what
I could of New York, until the sailing of the steamer. The
steamer anchored out in the harbour, and the passengers went on
board in a small tender, late in the evening Everything was in a
state of confusion, but I managed to get the key of my state-
room, put in my luggage, and later on went quietly to bed, awaken-
ing next morning to find we were some distance out of New York
harbour, in calm and delightful weather.

Isthmus of
ed the first
lor, at that
hat I could
five tier of
ugh to San
d up to the
but a happy
tion, and at
it train and
I went to
is in. His
ong." We
mpany was
Horn, to
nch at Rio
vay. This
of seeing
it passage.
I saw what
ner. The
s went on
was in a
my state-
, awaken-
New York

CHAPTER II.

We had beautiful weather all the way to Rio Janeiro, and in passing opposite the mouth of the Oronoco River, a long distance from land, it was easy to distinguish the line between the dirty looking water of the river and the beautiful clear ocean water. I found it very enjoyable at night, when the weather was warm, to stow myself away in a sail on the bowsprit and smoke, watching the beautiful phosphorescent sparks flying out of the ocean at every plunge of the ship. Two porpoises stationed themselves a few feet in front and on each side of the stem of the ship, and accompanied us for a long time.

With the passing days I began to find that we had a peculiar mixture of passengers, notably among whom was a band of the disgusting "free-lovers" from the state of Ohio, and I must say the "ladies" of that party were far from being angels in appearance, language, or manner. Many were the flirtations, and great the jealousy existing between two of our lady cabin passengers. One sultry afternoon, I was alone reading in the saloon close to the adjoining ladies' cabin, when I was somewhat astonished to hear through the open door remarkably forcible language, followed by what was evidently a fierce encounter. In I went and closed the door, to find the belligerents tugging away at each other's hair in a most fierce manner. Over went chairs and tables, but I could not separate the Amazons. The purser fortunately made his appearance on the scene; he seized hold of one, and I of the other, and by choking them pretty well, we managed to part them, when their language to each other was certainly not parliamentary. One bright and charming day we steamed into the magnificent harbour of Rio Janeiro, passing the large and apparently formidable fortifications on the north side of the narrow entrance that guards it. We anchored opposite the city, and here we were to remain some time to take in stores, &c. I therefore stayed on shore to see what I could of the city and suburbs. There were not any quays at that time, and the steamer had to lie at anchor in the bay, and load with lighters.

e that guards
remain some
e to see what
any quays at
the bay, and

CHAPTER III.

Taking my quarters up at an hotel that fronts the Plaza, I heard that yellow fever was raging. Then, as soon as the sun's rays were fading, I took a stroll. The city was greatly disappointing— its streets are narrow, the stores and houses of a very inferior description, and I mistook the Emperor's town residence for a jail. It was impossible to get a light cooling drink, and I concluded that if some one from Niagara Falls would undertake the business he would make a fortune. I saw some disgusting cases of what I supposed to be elephantiasis, as the parts affected were greatly swollen. Retiring early to bed, the fleas gave me not a moment's peace, and I was quickly obliged to change quarters for the night to a chair. I afterwards visited the market and rather admired the tropical fruits, as well as the tall and well-formed negresses, with their white dresses and turbans, who attend there. At the time of my visit I understood the slave trade was stopped as far as the importation of fresh slaves was concerned, but the old supply were still in slavery. It was amusing to see the strings of negroes performing work that in our cities is done with drays. They generally packed the loads on their heads. I took a trip to the small town of Botafoga, where there are some very pretty private residences and quantities of flowers. With the doctor of our ship I paid a visit to the Botanical Gardens, and could not but admire the fine avenues of trees. We went to the top of the "Coco Vada" overlooking the city and harbour, and commanding a beautiful and extensive view. Up this mountain the Emperor has built a good road, and it is well shaded with trees. My next visit was to an old and interesting monastery, where I tried to make out the epitaphs on the large flag-stones that cover the remains of the venerable fathers.

Hearing that the Emperor and Empress and Court were going to attend a service in a very pretty church, I went too. The shabby cavalry escort was surprising. Two rows of negro soldiers, about ten feet apart, with blue coats and brass buttons, armed with flint-lock muskets and fixed bayonets, stationed themselves along the aisle, and the Emperor, Empress, and Court walked up to the altar The Emperor is a fine, tall looking man ; the Empress appeared to me rather short and stout The court dresses were very pretty and tastefully worn. The hospital was the next building visited ; it is capitally managed, and has fine airy wards.

I was told a melancholy story. A Scotch gentleman had a large plantation in Brazil, and he brought out his young wife to his hacienda. One day when visiting a distant part of his estate, as he was travelling along a bush road in the heat of the day, everything still and motionless, he was astonished to see something swinging from the limb of a tree backwards and forwards across the road. He approached and there to his surprise lay an enormous serpent With his rifle he shot it through the head, and wishing to save the skin, dragged it back to his hacienda with the lasso. Thinking to astonish his wife, he coiled the serpent up in the drawing-room, taking it in through one of the glass doors that opened on to the verandah He then called his wife and went into another room Presently he heard some terrific screams and rushed in to find his wife in convulsions on the floor, and in a few minutes she was a corpse. Two small punctures were found on her breast, and a day or two afterwards one of his slaves discovered the mate of the dead serpent lying under the verandah, leading to the supposition that it followed the trail of its dead comrade, and reaching the room just when the unfortunate lady entered, killed her

The heat was so great that the short time I remained in Rio was principally occupied in smoking cigars and drinking brandy and water to keep away the yellow fever, which had become very bad.

The Doctor and myself having supplied ourselves with a good supply of port wine in long-necked bottles and some other luxuries, went aboard ship, and hung all the bottles with strings to battens in his surgery

s and brass
l bayonets,
or, Empress,
s a fine, tall
rt and stout.
worn. The
ly managed,

had a large
wife to his
his estate, as
of the day,
e something
vards across
ay an enor-
head, and
da with the
rpent np in
s doors that
e and went
screams and
r, and in a
re found on
s discovered
leading to
mrade, and
ered, killed

ied in Rio
ing brandy
ecome very

ith a good
r luxuries,
to battens

CHAPTER IV.

We left Rio for Magellan's Straits. On the way our ship encountered a tornado; one moment everything was as if we were in a blaze of fire, and the next in utter darkness. As I stood clinging to the mizzen-mast the ship would make a fearful plunge as if she never could rise again, but would seek the bottom of the ocean. The next day a most woful disappointment awaited my friend the doctor and I, for on entering the surgery to enjoy a glass of wine every jar was smashed, and the wine well mixed up on the floor with countless drugs.

We now entered the cold, dreary, and inhospitable Straits of Magellan, observing some old wrecks as we steamed along, and, passing the Chilian penal station, anchored in a cove near a Chilian brig of war. The strong head wind and adverse current detained us here a short time. Using this opportunity, I called on the Chilian officers, and heard from them how that the convicts had risen a short time previously and roasted the Governor of the penal settlement, and how the brig had been there to hunt them up; catching some, and others escaping.

One day I made a trip up the adjoining mountains, that rise abruptly on each side of the Straits, to get a good view. Pulling myself up to a ledge a terrific growl met my ears, and a fierce looking animal, about as big as a wolf, stood within six feet of my face. One hurried look was enough, and down I went that mountain with much greater speed than I had ascended it. A few natives were there camped in a miserable hut — small, wretched, filthy, and frightfully ugly creatures, quite nude, with the exception of a small piece of the skin of some animal over their shoulders. I tried to talk with them, but could make nothing of their signs. They kept pointing to my cap which, as my others had been blown overboard, was the last one I had—an old uniform cap of the Yorkville cavalry (of which I had been one of the officers)—of which some of the silver lace was visible, the oil-cloth covering being slightly displaced. I took it off to show it them, and my attention being drawn away for a few seconds I could see nothing more of it, though a figure was to be seen running up the beach of the cove. I immediately gave chase, and on nearing the little figure, into the water, only about three feet deep, it dashed, and I after it, as I saw my cap. I thus overtook the runaway, vowing fierce vengeance, and catching hold of the long coarse hair and my cap, was about to administer a sound flogging, when the captive proved to be a woman, so giving her a few plunges under the water, which might have washed off a little of her filth, we waded amicably ashore, she grinning as if in enjoyment of the sport.

The ship now made a start and steamed away until 4 p.m., but could make no anchorage, so the captain turned about, and in an hour's time we were again at our old anchorage. Matters now became a little serious, as both fuel and provisions were not over plentiful, and the captain thought if the strong wind lasted he must go back and round the "Horn." But fortunately the wind went down on the next day and we entered the Pacific, only to meet another gale, which, together with a strong southerly current, swept us along the coast of Terra del Fuego (the land of fires). That night as I stood alongside the captain for some hours holding on to the mizzen-mast, it seemed as though I should see the last of our steamer *Hermann* and her crew and passengers. The bleak rocky cliffs were in very close proximity to the vessel's stern, and with all the steam we could put on we could not move ahead an inch, but fortunately the wind fell, and we got off and had a pleasant run along the coast of Chili to Coronel and Lota, where we stopped to coal and get a few supplies.

CHAPTER V.

During the time occupied in coaling, some eighty of us, with our captain, made a trip to Conception, about twenty-five miles distant; the American Consul, who was a splendid fellow, accompanying us. Some went in carriages and some on horseback. I was fortunate in getting a good horse and enjoyed the trip. It is generally known how the old city of Conception was destroyed by an earthquake; I regret I had not time to visit it. On crossing the Bio Bio River we came to the present city, and found it but a small place. The houses generally were of low build to guard against earthquakes, with not too many windows facing the streets, for rebellions were not uncommon. We put up at a very fair hotel kept by an American, whose name has escaped my memory. In the evening we all went to the theatre, but not understanding the language we repaired to a large building, and having engaged a small band and such of the Peon damsels as we could pick up, we had a ball and gave them all a supper. It was here I first saw the graceful South American dance—the Zemba Queca (I am not certain how it is spelt). We enjoyed the night, and next morning returned. On my way I was exceedingly thirsty, and being in the rear with a jovial companion, we went to a house we saw some distance off the road. This we found to be a wayside inn, and the sight of rows of bottles of Allsop's ale and huge butts of native wine was most cheering. Unfortunately my companion took a little too much, and I had great difficulty in getting him on his horse, but I succeeded, and to keep him there tied a rope to his feet and passed it under the horse's belly. By riding alongside and holding him we were enabled to reach our destination, but as I was on the point of going down the long wharf two fellows stopped me, and tried to make me pay for someone else's horse they said had not been settled for. The

last boat was holding on with a boat hook to the wharf for
me, so to bring the matter to an end I jumped down about
eight feet into her, and wished the two Peons a long and last
farewell.

The run to Valparaiso was pleasant. We remained but a short
time, and I had not the opportunity of visiting San Jago or
Santiago, which I now regret. The open roadstead at Valparaiso
conveys the idea that the harbour is not the best. The city itself
is not conspicuous for fine hotels, nor for handsome houses. There
are three hills, known as the Fore, Main, and Mizzen tops, but
I had not the opportunity of learning much about the place.
Here we were joined by a very pleasant Irish gentleman from
Australia, a Mr. O'Rafferty, who had been on a mercantile tour.
Sailing for the Bay of Panama, we anchored at the island of
Tobago, some nine miles from the city of Panama. We here
heard that the vessel was likely to be seized, but a bottomry
bond was given and our captain left us to go back to New York,
leaving the vessel in command of the chief officer. I may here
say that Captain Cavendy was a fine fellow, a gentleman and
thorough seaman, and his loss was regretted by all on board.
We had a pleasant run to San Francisco, but before the anchor
was down the ship was seized and we were all turned ashore.
My passage through to Victoria being lost, I was now in a
dilemma; all the money I had left was two dollars and a half.
I was unknown in San Francisco, and to make matters worse
the steamer for Victoria did not leave for a day or two.
Fortunately I was able to do a good turn for my Australian
friend, and he paid my expenses in San Francisco, making me
a capital offer to go to Melbourne, but I was too much bent
upon my original plan to turn aside. I saw Captain Dall, of the
steamer *Panama*, and, explaining my position to him, he most
kindly offered me a first-class passage, to be paid for when
convenient.

ie wharf for
down about
ong and last
d but a short
San Jago or
at Valparaiso
The city itself
ouses. There
zen tops, but
ut the place
itleman from
rcantile tour
the island o
i. We her
a bottomry
to New York
I may here
intleman and
all on board
re the anche
irned ashore
is now in
s and a half
iatters worse
day or two
iy Australia
i, making m
o much beu
n Dall, of th
him, he moe
aid for whe

CHAPTER VI.

Steaming away for Victoria the passage was rough and most disagreeable. The vessel had no comforts, and the rain and sleet blew into my state-room on the upper deck. The steamer was crowded and cold, a family of Oregonians keeping so close to the little stove in the saloon as to make it impossible to get near it; we named them "The Happy Family." I was accustomed to put on my overcoat and riding boots when I went to bed to try and keep dry and warm. We ran into the Columbia River, passed the celebrated "Astoria," and stuck fast on a mud bar at "Warrior Point." A small steamer from Portland came and took off the passengers and cargo destined for that city, and we managed to get off with the next tide. Seeing numerous wild fowl in the river and on the mud flats along its banks, I landed and succeeded in killing a number of them. On my return to the steamer I went to my state-room to get a glass of whisky and a cigar—(my Australian friend had presented me with two gallons and a box of cigars on my leaving San Francisco)—but to my horror found they had disappeared, together with two bags containing many articles of clothing and nearly all my supply of boots, a most serious loss when my pockets were empty. I found the waiter who attended the state-room had left by the steamer for Portland, and some uncharitable thoughts passed through my mind regarding his sense of honesty. We continued our journey, the weather still keeping stormy and disagreeable, and visited Puget Sound, touching at several of the small towns, but the rain and fogs allowed one to see but little of the sound. I noticed it was densely covered with very fine timber—principally the "Douglas fir," and the numerous Indian log canoes I saw of different sizes and shapes were beautifully modelled and capital sea canoes. I was astonished at the enormous size of some of them made out of single logs. A few more hours brought us to Esquimault Harbour, the naval station in British Columbia, about three miles from Victoria.

CHAPTER VII.

I was very favourably impressed with the harbour of Esquimault and its immediate surroundings, and though the day was misty and disagreable I could not but notice the many beauties of the harbour. Wishing good-bye to my friend Captain Dall, I walked to Victoria over a very muddy road. Passing through the Indian village opposite Victoria, curiosity prompted me to enter some of the houses. I was struck with their great size, the indescribable filth of both houses and occupants, and the frightful flat heads of the Indians, so well described to me and illustrated in his paintings by my friend Mr. Paul Kane. Crossing a long bridge over the arm of the sea that forms the harbour of Victoria, I entered that city, and walking up Yates-street, I saw a wooden hotel which I entered, and found it crowded with miners clad in their rough garments and occupied in discussing the mines, their adventures, &c., in the very expressive language then in vogue amongst the early prospectors of the country. Having succeeded in securing a bed in a double room—or, rather, den—and refreshing myself with a meal and smoke, I took a walk through the rather muddy streets to see the town, which, at that time, seemed much overcrowded. From what I could gather from the miners who had returned from the Fraser River, the prospects of going to the interior at that time of the year were most discouraging. The following morning I walked over to Sir James Douglas' residence, and met him as he was on the point of going to his office. Sir James received me most kindly, and when I had presented my letter of introduction from Sir George Simpson, he asked me to call upon him at his office at 1 o'clock p.m., which I did, and he at once offered me an appointment in the Government service. This offer, after fully explaining to him my views and the object I had in coming to the country, I very courteously declined. Sir James

Esquimault
s misty and
ties of the
ll, I walked
arongh the
ne to enter
it size, the
he frightful
lustrated in
ing a long
of Victoria,
w a wooden
miners clad
the mines,
go then in
y. Having
ther, den—
ok a walk
iich, at that
gather from
he prospects
were most
ver to Sir
n the point
most kindly,
on from Sir
at his office
fered me an
offer, after
t I had in
Sir James

said, "My dear Moberly, you have no idea of the enormous trees and rocks you will have to encounter, to say nothing of the severe weather that is coming on, but come and take a plate of soup with me at half-past six this evening, and I will have leisure to give you some information about British Columbia." At the appointed time I reached the Governor's house, and he introduced me to his kind and interesting family. I also had the pleasure of meeting Judge Begbie—now Sir Matthew Bailey Begbie, Chief Justice of British Columbia—Mr. Dallas, Dr. Helmcken, Mr. Donald Fraser, and others. I found the "plate of soup" was a capital dinner, and I have pleasure in recalling that evening to memory as one of the most enjoyable I ever spent, and the vast amount of information about British Columbia and the Pacific Coast given me by Sir James was afterwards invaluable. From that time until the day of his death I found Sir James always a kind and hospitable friend, and it is now a matter of history that he was an able and honourable Governor. I returned to my den, packed my blankets and a few things, and went on board the Hudson Bay Company's steamer *Otter*, bound for Fort Langley on the Fraser River.

CHAPTER VIII.

The trip from Victoria to Fort Langley was not pleasant, as the weather was boisterous and rainy, and the steamer crowded. On reaching Fort Langley a most hospitable reception awaited me from Chief Factor Yale, then—and, as he afterwards informed me, for thirty years previous—in charge of that large and important fort. I here met with several of the officers of the company, all of whom were most kind and gave me a great deal of information. The following day the little steamer *Enterprise* (Capt. Tom Wright) started up the Fraser for Fort Yale, and I took passage on her. As a number of passengers were struggling through the mud to get on board, we were greatly encouraged by the captain's words, in blowing the last whistle, "Hurry up, boys, as the steamer is going to blow up in forty seconds, and I can't wait." About noon next day, after a passage made disagreeable by the rain and snow and crowded steamer, a number of us got off at the Indian village at the mouth of the Harrison River, the *Enterprise* going on by the Fraser to Fort Yale. We here heard rumours of a war having broken out between the Indians and miners on the Fraser somewhere above Yale. I then packed my blankets into a large Indian house or rancherie close at hand, to get out of the snow and rain, and a trader, who wanted to send a large canoe of goods and whisky up to Port Douglas, said if I could "raise" a crew, and take charge of the goods, we should feed ourselves out of the cargo and make our way over Harrison Lake, which is some forty miles in length. I collected a crew in a few minutes, but they proved *a bad crew*. We poled the canoe up to the rapids, a short distance below Harrison Lake. Here night overtook us when opposite an Indian village, composed of several large rancheries, and a few hundred Indians. The evening was cold, wet, and gloomy, and the river banks low and swampy. I ran the bow of the canoe into one of the little doors of a large house.

The Indians cleared a corner for us, and made a small fire at which we cooked some bacon, &c., and having brought our cargo in we lay down on some mats around the fire. What with the stories I had heard of the Indians, and the cargo of whisky with me, I could not sleep, expecting to be murdered at any moment. I lay with my overcoat over me, facing the numerous fires in all parts of the building, around which the Indians were sleeping, and with my revolver in my hand felt ready for any emergency. The fires were gradually going out, with the exception of our own, when I saw a tall Indian rise out of his blankets, clad only in a shirt, and taking a careful look all around, advance in our direction, stepping carefully over the sleeping forms of the intervening Indians, and holding his hands behind him. I thought it was all "up" with us, for I imagined he had a knife in his hand, so I cocked my revolver in readiness to shoot. He came to the fire, took a careful look at us and quietly turned round to warm his back, when I saw he had only a pipe in his hand, instead of the dreaded knife. That Indian had a narrow escape, and so had we, for had I shot him we should not have been alive many seconds. I rose and offered the Indian a piece of tobacco, and he then went away and brought me a piece of dried salmon, which I ate, and we became very good friends, so far, at least, as we could, for neither of us understood a word the other said. The next and two following days we made very bad headway against a strong wind, but at last arrived at the little stream connecting the small circular lake, upon which Port Douglas is situate, with the north end of Harrison Lake. On entering the stream we ran against the sharp edge of some newly-formed ice and split the bow of our log canoe, which caused it to sink almost immediately. The crew shouldered their blankets, and left me with a young lad to do the best we could with the cargo and ourselves. I managed to get hold of some Indians who were passing, and engaged them to pack the cargo to the trader's store, myself taking up quarters in a long wooden building with a bar at one end, and miners and packers drinking and gambling all round the room.

CHAPTER IX.

In the morning I managed to hire an Indian to pack my blankets, &c., over the twenty-nine mile portage by a trail opened by the Government in the previous autumn at great cost. The snow was very deep and the trail unbroken. After toiling for a long time through the snow we reached the top of a hill that commands a view up the foaming Lillovet River for some distance, when my Indian sat down and we both had a smoke and rest. He tried to explain something to me, but I could not understand him ; so when I thought we had rested long enough, I took the pack and put it on his back, at which he grew very indignant, talking away in an excited manner, pointing up the river, and at last flinging my pack down and leaving me. There was now nothing for me to do but pack it myself, so I accordingly shouldered it and tried to get along. After an hour's excessively hard work I found I had made hardly any headway, and despaired of getting through. To go on was formidable, to turn back ignominious, so I abandoned the pack, taking my overcoat and a few things out of it, and left it for the first comer. I passed some fine white pine, being the first I had seen in the country. Pushing on, I reached some fine hot springs and a shanty with one white man in it. I had a bath and slept on some brush, and next morning resumed my journey, reaching Lillovet Lake, where I again got into a log hut of small size. The following day I got a passage over Lake Lillovet in considera-tion of rowing an oar, crossing the other lakes and portages in a similar manner, and arriving in the afternoon of a fine clear day on the flat where the present town of Lillovet is built. The scenery here was very fine, and I pushed on, passing the mouth of Bridge River and reached a store at the " Fountain." There I met some miners, and we agreed to form a mining partnership, go up a few miles and work a bar upon which they said they had found

good prospects. Our combined resources were limited, and the price
of provisions excessively high. We secured an outfit and reached the
scene of our anticipated fortunes the same evening, sleeping in the
soft deep snow, which was warm and comfortable. The following
day we made a very diminutive hut out of stones, logs, and snow,
and my companions, who were old hands at mining, made a
"rocker." The weather was cold, the ground frozen like iron
and covered with snow, and my occupation was to climb some
fifteen hundred feet up an adjacent mountain and cut trees and
roll the logs down for the others to thaw the frozen ground, and
wash the "dirt." Owing to the severe weather we could make very
little progress, and our scanty stock of provisions was about consumed: our appetites increasing as supplies decreased. We concluded
to put all our remaining resources together, get what we could in the
shape of provisions at the "Fountain," and endeavour to hold out
until the spring thaw set in. One of my companions and myself
went to the little store, and obtaining a very small supply of provisions returned to camp. We now put ourselves on short rations,
but at last everything was eaten up, and still no appearance of
a change in the weather. We were now regularly starved out and
"dead broke," so when the sun rose on a clear and cold day we
adandoned our hut, mine, &c., and began our retreat down the
Fraser River, walking partly on the ice and partly on the
banks. At the mouth of Bridge River my companions left me,
intending to go down to the fork of the Fraser and Thompson
Rivers (Lytton), where paying mining was going on, I retracing my
steps by the Harrison-Lillovet trail. That was, indeed, a hungry
day. In the afternoon, when walking along a high "bench" of
the river, I saw smoke arising from the river bottom and soon
caught sight of a camp with a newly-slaughtered animal hanging
on a neighbouring tree. I slid and scrambled down the steep bank
and made a rush for the carcass, from which I cut a good slice, and
coming to the fire, much to the amusement of the men sitting
there, told them I was starving and bound to have a meal but
could not pay for it. They brought out a pan of fried bacon and
beans, a pot of coffee and some slap jacks, all of which I devoured

with my slice of meat, and then they produced some tobacco, and I felt happy. Wishing my charitable hosts good day, I resumed my journey and reached the head of Seaton Lake, where I found three boatmen preparing for the freight they expected would arrive shortly from Port Douglas, and as two of them wanted to get a boat over from the Fraser River into the lake, I made a bargain to help the third to get a big scow over the lake for my passage and meals. The next day and a portion of the night was spent in tugging away at an enormous oar, and we got to another station kept by other boatmen in partnership with my friends. Here we had our night's rest, and before daylight I left for a long walk over the twenty-four mile portage.

o, and
sumed
found
would
ted to
ıade a
ke for
: night
got to
ith my
: I left

CHAPTER X.

The snow was deep, the trail through it narrow, and rain and subsequent frost had made the bottom of the track rough and icy, I reached the lower end with very sore feet some hours after dark, and, passing a cabin, went a short distance to the lake, where I had noticed a hut on my way up. Into this I went, and finding a heap of shavings in the corner commenced to knock them into a good pile, when I was astonished to find my proposed bed already occupied by a miner on his way down, in the same predicament as myself. We lit a fire, had a smoke and talk, and then lay down in the shavings. The worst news I gathered from him was that the boat or canoe would not be in on the following day. In the morning I was washing my face in the snow, when a tall fellow, followed by a " greaser " (the name given to Mexican-Indian half-breeds), passed, and saluted us by the following :—

" Don't you men want a job? I have a scow of provisions in and want it unloaded, and will give you each two dollars and a half to do it." I replied, " Will you give us a breakfast, too ?" Answer—" Yes ; come along."

We went down, cooked our grub on the beach, and eat such a meal as one does when he has a tremendous appetite, and thinks he may never have another chance. We did the work and got our pay, with a little tobacco as a bonus, and then returned to our cabin. During the forenoon I was cleaning my revolver, when a man, dressed in a large canvas overshirt with a huge red beard, made his appearance, and eyeing my revolver said, " Cap., what sort of a shooting iron is that ?" He pulled out a Colt's navy revolver, and said he would shoot a match with me for two dollars and a half a shot. I thought of my solitary two and a half I had made in the morning, and concluded to accept the challenge. We accordingly made a mark on a tree, tossed up for first turn, which he won, and when he fired made a very bad shot. I won some five or six in succession, and when I had about enough to pay my way down I thought it time to stop ; besides I was afraid he might not pay me, so I suggested the advisability of our stopping, to which he agreed, saying I could beat him. He now asked me to come with him to the little groggery he was staying at and have a drink, I wondering if he would pay me. After we had a drink he pulled out a long bag of gold dust and told the man to weigh out for me seventy-five dollars, to take the price of the drinks, and let him have a bottle of whisky, for which the charge was sixteen dollars. I got some crackers and sardines and we rejoined my friend at the hut, and spent the rest of the day telling of our mining adventures, &c. This fortunate windfall enabled me to reach Fort Langley in a few days, where I met my old acquaintance, Captain Tom Wright, and as his steamer was beached for repairs he very kindly asked me to stay on board with him until the Victoria steamer arrived. During my stay with Captain Wright we made a trip up the " Pitt River" and Lake to see if there was a chance to get communication with the Douglas portages, and on my return went to Victoria, rather at a loss what to do next.

ssed up
ry bad
I had
o stop;
ed the
I could
e little
g if he
ng bag
ity-five
a bottle
t some
ut, and
res, &c.
ey in a
Wright,
ked me
arrived.
e " Pitt
mmuni-
ent to

CHAPTER XI.

On my return to Victoria I called at Sir James Douglas' office,
and in the ante-room met Judge Begbie, whom I had previously
met at the Governor's. By him I was introduced to a gentleman
who happened to come in : he turned out to be Colonel R.
C. Moody, in command of the Royal Engineers, who had
arrived in the country after I left for the interior. I had a
short conversation with him, and he invited me to see him at
his quarters. After a long interview with Sir James Douglas,
when I gave him particulars of the country, and of what he
was most anxious to know—the feasibility of building a waggon
road over the Harrison-Lillovet trail—he strongly recommended
me to remain in the colony and turn my attention to the construction of the trails and roads that were certain to be made as soon
as possible. On my way from Sir James' office I met Colonel
and Mrs. Moody. The former asked me to his quarters, where I
at once went, and before I left had offered me an appointment
to be attached to the corps of Royal Engineers in a civil capacity.
The second day afterwards I returned with Colonel Moody to
Langley and thence to " Derby," where I met Captain J. Grant
and the other officers of the Royal Engineers. The next morning
Colonel Moody wished me to go down the river to the proposed
new city, and getting a week's rations, a tent, and picking up
a man and an old leaky boat, I tied her to the steamer *Beaver*
as she ran down the river, and we were shortly on shore at the
site proposed. The trees, as a general thing, were of enormous
size, and the underbrush dense. We made a little pathway for
a few hundred feet and came to a magnificent bird's-eye maple
tree, under which I pitched the tent, and founded the city of
Queenborough, now known as New Westminster. Snow was still
in the bush, but the weather was fine. I looked about through

the woods and found that a great deal of work would be required to clear away the timber. The next day I sent up an order to Derby for supplies, tools, and fifty men, and the following day they arrived, some in boats, others on rafts, and I organised my camp. I was busy for some time, during which the various Government buildings were erected, the survey of the city made, and the first sale of lots took place in Victoria. An amusing incident happened one day: I had been up to the "Camp," which is some distance above the city, and on my return found the whole place in a state of great excitement and all classes very much excited, as coarse gold was supposed to be discovered in a little stream that flowed alongside my cabin. The unfortunate stream was likely to be dug away, when it turned out that the "coarse gold" was nothing but spelter some wicked-minded individual had thrown in, and the "sell" was very great. It was a hard matter afterwards to get anyone to admit that he had prospected *on that creek.*

The supply of fish was very plentiful, the salmon, of which there are two species—the red and the white—being in enormous quantities. The sturgeon attain to a great size. There is a small and most delicate fish known as the "Oolahan," that comes in May and remains a short time. It is about the size of a sardine and very rich, delicate, and oily. The salmon will not take the fly on the Pacific Coast. There are oysters, mussels, clams, crabs, prawns, &c., &c., but I never heard of a lobster being found anywhere on the Pacific Coast. Red deer were formerly very numerous on the islands in the Gulf of Georgia, and are still so on Vancouver Island. The panther and bear were also to be found on the island. Many wild berries abounded in the woods, and some of them were pleasant to the taste.

CHAPTER XII.

Shortly after the sale of the lots I left the Government service and went to explore Burrard Inlet for coal, &c. Mr. Robert Burnaby, formerly private secretary to Colonel Moody, accompanying me with a few men. We spent some time there, and were for a short time in the position of hostages with the Indians. Making a trip up the north arm, we camped on a rocky point and tied our canoe to a tree, only partially hauling her on the rock. Burnaby and I slept in the canoe, and I awoke with an unpleasant sensation, finding my feet were much higher than my head. I could not understand the situation at all, but could see Burnaby fast asleep at the other end of the canoe, which would apparently be soon standing on end. Satisfying myself that I was not dreaming, I crawled carefully to the other end, when the canoe suddenly resumed its horizontal position and Burnaby awoke. We found when we went to bed that the tide was in, but as it ran out of course the canoe kept tilting over, and we had but narrowly escaped a bath a little before our usual hour. I was impressed with the magnificent harbour and the many natural advantages for building up an immense city. Abundance of good water power also, which will doubtless be of great value in the course of time.

Learning from the Indians that gold had been discovered up the Squamish River, which empties into the head of Howe Sound, and prompted by a desire to see as much of the country as possible, Burnaby and I left our men to prosecute the work of sinking shafts, while we made a trip up the sound and river. The shores of Howe Sound we found sterile and barren, and the current in the Squamish River strong. At the point where the Jeakniss River forms a junction with the Squamish River we left our canoe in charge of a young Indian chief, and crossing a portage obtained a small canoe for our journey up the lesser stream. At the juncture of the rivers was a large settlement of

Indians, probably 2,500 in number, with several of the large Indian houses, and at the upper end of the portage lay a smaller village. We went some distance up stream with the canoe, where the water getting shallow and very swift we pushed forward on foot, reaching at nightfall the place where the gold was supposed to be. One of the Indians pointed out with great satisfaction a prospecting hole about eight feet in depth, and a blazed tree with some writing on it. The writing on the tree was the work of some miners who had prospected the river the year before, and it informed us that they had been quite unsuccessful. We had a good laugh and camped, then retraced our steps, made our friend the Indian chief a present and ran back to Burrard Inlet. The timber along the river was very fine and wild berries plentiful. At this spot I met an old acquaintance. Hearing the sound of an axe a short distance in the woods I went there and found a large, powerful Indian, who at once put his axe down, and came up and gave me a kiss on the fore-head, shaking my hand in a most hearty manner. I could at first understand what it was all about until he pulled out a curious dirk-knife, which I remembered giving an Indian, with some other articles, when I was at Westminster the year before. He made me a present of some dried bear's meat, and I gave him a piece of tobacco. Always give a present to an Indian if he gives you one, for he expects it. Another rather curious circumstance occurred as we were going up the river. In a long, shallow slough, formed by a gravel bar, which the falling water had left dry, the Indians pointed out a curious ripple, and called out, " Hyas salmon," which is a very big salmon. We all got out with the poles and paddles, and forming a line across the water gradually drove the salmon to the upper end of the enclosure. Here we thought we should get him, but to our astonishment he made a sudden rush, and with a leap to the dry bar, and still another leap, went clear into the main river—was that instinct or accident ? As we found we had not proper machinery to carry on our prospecting for coal we gave it up, and returned to New Westminster, shortly afterwards going to Victoria for the winter.

large
naller
where
.rd on
.posed
action
.l tree
work
.efore,
. We
made
.urrard
.l wild
.tance·
woods
. once
. ·.re-
.t
.urious
. other
made
.iece of
.u one,
.curred
.formed
.ndians
.lmon,"
.es and
.ve the
ght we
n rush,
.t clear
As we
.pecting
shortly

CHAPTER XIII.

During the winter of 1859-60 I tried hard to promote a
company to build a tramway from Victoria to Esquimault, but
without success. This winter I had the pleasure and good fortune
to meet Captain Palliser, Dr. Hector, Mr. Sullivan, and others
connected with that well-known exploration in British North
America, and gained much valuable information of the prairie
country, and such portions of the mountain ranges as they
had traversed. In the spring I went back to New Westminster,
and surveyed and took up the south side of English Bay,
Burrard Inlet, and both sides of Port Moody. On my return to
Westminster I entered into a contract, in partnership with Mr.
Edgar Dewdney, to build a trail from Fort Hope on the Fraser
River to the Shemilkomean River on the east side of the
Cascade range of mountains, to reach the gold-diggings on the
latter river, where gold of a very fine quality had been discovered. Meeting with a very severe accident, I was laid up
for some days in a miserable swamp, with only an Indian boy
for my companion, and when I felt a little better I rode a mule
down to a small log store-house which we had at a little
lake. I arrived in the evening, and soon lay down to rest in
the lower of two bunks in one corner of the house. As I lay
there, watching the moon shining through a large square
opening in the roof that served the purpose of a chimney, I heard
something walking on the mud-covered roof, and quietly got up
with my revolver. I thought it might be an Indian, intent on
stealing some of our supplies, or rum, of which we kept a good
quantity in this house. I saw what I took to be a hand carefully
come down through the opening, evidently feeling what was
below. This was repeated several times, when I managed to get
into such a position as to leave the moonbeam between myself and

invader, when, instead of an Indian, I made it out to be a large panther—an animal very scarce on the mainland, but more plentiful on Vancouver Island. This made me feel uncomfortable, and, as soon as the moonlight came between us I fired, and as I found in the morning by some blood on the roof, must have hit the brute. For the rest of that night I occupied the upper bunk, and barricaded it with tobacco boxes, my sleep not being very sound. When the work was drawing to a close I went over to the Shemilkomean, where I had sent some surplus stores to sell to the miners—starting at the persuasion of a person who had opened a house at the Red Earth Forks of the Shemilkomean, and who had stayed a day or two at one of my camps, departing in great good humour, as I had given him a small keg of my best H.B. Company's rum. I reached the mining camp, and went to my friend's house, six miles further on, where I made the acquaintance of one of the first Gold Commissioners of British Columbia. We passed a pleasant evening, drank several glasses of the rum I had given the proprietor of the house and consumed some fresh eggs. On leaving in the morning I was at a loss to know whether to offer to pay for my night's entertainment or not, as I was an invited guest. However, I suggested in a delicate manner that in such a country it was necessary to pay. My landlord, my supposed host, without hesitation produced a slate with my bill already made out : meals, 2 dollars 50 cents each ; drinks, 50 cents each ; the confounded eggs 1 dollar apiece, and 75 cents per pound for the barley for my horse. I paid the bill and jumped on my horse, vowing it would be some time before I accepted another invitation or enjoyed the luxury of fresh eggs.

large
more
mfort-
d, and
t have
upper
being
t over
to sell
ho had
n, and
ting in
 my best
went
made
ners of
several
house
orning
night's
ever, I
it was
hesita-
meals, 2
ounded
for my
ving it
tion or

MOUNT STEPHEN, IN THE CANADIAN ROCKY MOUNTAINS, AND THE RIVER LAGGAN,
ON THE LINE OF THE CANADIAN PACIFIC RAILWAY.

CHAPTER XIV.

A.D. 1861.—The gold mines on the Shemilkomean and at "Rock Creek," which is further to the eastward, having yielded good returns in the autumn, Sir James Douglas visited them personally, going by way of Kamloops and Okawajau lake, and on his return came over the trail we had then nearly completed. Sir James was anxious to construct a waggon-road without loss of time over the same route as that followed by the trail, and requested me to meet him at Victoria as soon as I could get down after the trail was completed. In the early part of the winter I went down, and it was arranged that we should construct the westerly portion of the waggon-road, Captain Grant, with a detachment of the Royal Engineers, assisting with a force of civilian labour in the easterly part. In the spring, on the opening of navigation, both of our forces went to work and continued until the winter set in, opening an eighteen-foot waggon-road over the heaviest part of the work. It was during this summer that the celebrated Cariboo mines were struck, and the enormous yield in them in a few weeks at the close of the season attracted the attention of the whole colony from "Qutter" and "Williams" creeks. The miners on the Shemilkomean abandoned that section of the country for the more promising one at Cariboo. Sir James Douglas very wisely decided to husband all the resources of the colony, which were very limited, and with his usual indomitable energy and determination constructed a first-class waggon-road into Cariboo. During the past two seasons a waggon-road had been in course of construction from Port Douglas to Lillovet, Mr. Joseph William Trutch doing the larger portion of the work. Several companies applied for charters to build trails and roads to the Cariboo mines, and charters were granted for trails from Bentinck Arm and Bute Inlet to Quesnel, and for waggon-roads from Lillovet to Clinton, and from Lytton to the same point and thence by a joint road to Fort Alexandria. I strongly urged upon Sir James Douglas the construction of the Fraser River road, as being the great natural and commercial artery of the country, and the probability of its becoming at some period in the future the line for a railway from Canada. Colonel Moody was already well acquainted with my views regarding the Fraser River route.

A.D. 1862.—It was finally settled that the Government, with the Royal Engineers and a force of civilians, should build the portion from Yale, the head of steamboat navigation on the Fraser River, to Chapman's Bar; Mr. Trutch the next section, by contract, to Boston Bar; Mr. Thomas Spence from Boston Bar to Lytton; and myself and two others the road from Lytton to Clinton under a charter contract, the payments to be partly in money and partly in tolls. Considering our limited resources we had undertaken a gigantic work, and during that and the following year, after many mishaps and changes, the great waggon-road was completed and placed in the hands of the Government, who levied a toll to repay in part the heavy outlay incurred. The season of 1863 was principally engaged in finishing portions of the waggon-road along the Thompson and Bonaparte rivers and Maiden Creek, and I wintered in Victoria.

Sir James Douglas told me the following story which gave the name to Maiden Creek :—" In the misty times of the past there was an Indian maiden who lived here with her tribe, and was engaged to be married to a young Indian chief who was a great warrior and hunter, and with whom she was deeply in love. He went on a long hunting expedition, and remained away all the winter, the maiden anxiously awaiting his return, as they were to have been married that winter. Spring came, and the maiden still sat watching for her absent lover near the junction of the creek with the Bonaparte River. After weary months he came bringing with him a wife from some distant tribe which he had visited. The poor maiden died of grief, and her tribe buried her at the mouth of the creek, the two little mounds or hillocks growing from her breasts and forming the two curious knolls that may be seen at this place."

CHAPTER XV.

A.D. 1864.—This year my old f ' end Sir James Douglas retired from office, and it was with feelings of great regret that I wished him good-bye on the morning of his departure from New Westminster. Sir James was succeeded by Mr. Frederic Seymour, and I went to Cariboo to look after the construction of the waggon road and other work undertaken by the Government in that portion of the country. I was simply appointed as Government engineer, and in the autumn, as the first Legislative Council was to be formed and rich gold fields had been discovered on Wild Horse Creek in the Kootanie District, I decided to resign my position and become elected for "Cariboo East," both of which I did, and attended the Council of 1864-5 at New Westminster. From my knowledge of the country I was of some service to Governor Seymour, and availed myself of the opportunity offered to impress upon him the vast importance to the colony of a good line for a waggon road and railway eastward of Kamloops. My views were supported by the Honourable Joseph William Trutch, who, about that time, was appointed Chief Commissioner of Lands and Works and Surveyor-General, and I was appointed his assistant.

A.D. 1865.—Resigning my seat in the Legislative Council, I was at once instructed to put such works into shape as were then in progress, and to take charge of the explorations and other works proposed to be undertaken east of Kamloops and extending to the easterly boundary of British Columbia, which, for a long distance north of the 49° parallel of latitude as far as the circle of longitude 126° west, is defined by the watershed of the Rocky Mountains. I now had my long wished-for opportunity to explore the Gold, Selkirk, and Rocky Mountains for a line suitable for an overland railway. No time was lost, and with a light exploring party I in a short time reached the Great Shuswap Lake, with a party of Shuswap Indians engaged to pack supplies from the head of the north arm to the Columbia River. I made a hurried trip to the south arm of the Great Shuswap Lake, noticing a valley running easterly apparently through the Gold range exactly in the direction in which I wished to find a pass. I went up the river a short distance, but had not the time at my disposal just then to examine it, having to see my party, &c., over to the Columbia River.

The following is quoted from my report of February 24th, 1872, to Mr. Sandford Fleming, Engineer-in-Chief, Canadian Pacific Railway, showing how the "Eagle Pass" derived its name from the following circumstances :—"In the summer of 1865, I was exploring the Gold range of mountains for the Government of British Columbia, to see if there was any pass through them. I arrived at the Eagle River, and on the top of a tree near its mouth I saw a nest full of eaglets, and the two old birds on a limb of the same tree. I had nothing but a small revolver in the shape of firearms ; this I discharged eight or ten times at the nest, but could not knock it down. The two old birds, after circling around the nest, flew up the valley of the river ; it struck me then, if I followed them, I might find the much wished-for pass. I explored the valley two or three weeks afterwards, and having been successful in finding a good pass, I thought the most appropriate name I could give it was the 'Eagle Pass.'"

I now returned to the head of the Shuswap Lake, rejoined my party and began our trip through the woods and over the Gold range to the Columbia River. About noon we stopped for lunch, and on my telling the Indians to go on they informed me their chief had given orders for them to camp there for the night. This was most provoking : the chief had gone off to hunt, and the Indians would not move ; so taking Perry, "the mountaineer" (he was well known in British Columbia, and afterwards killed by an Indian when asleep in his blankets under a tree at Burrard Inlet : he had a great dislike to Indians, and I often told him one would some day kill him), and an Indian boy with me, I camped on "The Summit." We killed ground hogs for our supper, and slept on some brush without blankets. The next day we reached the Columbia River early in the day, and commenced to make a log canoe to run the Columbia to the Arrow Lakes. On our way, being a few feet in front of Perry, I saw a big animal rise up on the opposite side of a fallen tree, and said to Perry, "Why, here is a cow"—(the brush was thick). Perry said "A grizzly!" The animal came towards us very quietly, and when a few feet off, Perry whistled, and the bear stood up on his hind legs, when Perry put a bullet through his heart and killed him. The animal being very lean and the skin worthless, we left it. Our canoe made good progress, and the Indians arrived, having eaten nearly all the provisions on the trip over. They had a grand war dance which lasted through the night, they being, as I learnt from them, at that time at war with the Columbia River Indians; their system being to murder each other in any manner when they meet. It was now apparent that I must get rid of the chief, while keeping the Indians in good humour, and as I wished to send a report to the Government, I informed the chief that I could entrust such an important document to no person but himself. I wished him to take it down to Kamloops, to which place he would go by canoe, and told him that on presenting a letter which I gave him at the Fort he would be provided with a horse and outfit to go on to Lytton, where he would receive further instructions from a friend of mine, to whom I also wrote, explaining my position and requesting him to treat the chief with all consideration, but to delay him as long as possible, so as to enable me to get away into the Selkirk Mountains before his return. I thus got rid in an amicable manner of a most troublesome companion, while the mission on which he went added much to his self-importance, and his Indians were delighted. I sent the Indians back for more supplies, and launching our little log canoe embarked for the run down the Columbia. We were swept along at a grand rate, and at last found the river getting narrow, with high rocky banks and overhanging cliffs. I was in the middle of the canoe taking bearings, estimating distances, &c., the Indian boy in the bow, and Perry steering. The boy suddenly exclaimed "Wake closhe

next day
mmenced
Lakes.
w a big
I said to
'erry said
nd when
his hind
led him.
e left it.
I, having
y had a
ing, as I
ia River
manner
id of the
I wished
f that I
but him-
place he
er which
nd outfit
ns from
tion and
, but to
way into
d in an
hile the
ortance,
for more
the run
ate, and
nks and
taking
he bow,
e closhe

chuck,--konaway namelnee," which is "bad water—all will be killed;" he put in his paddle and lay down in the bottom of the canoe. I crawled over him, and getting hold of the paddle Perry and I managed to keep the canoe out of the whirls, &c., that threatened to suck us down. At one moment we were on the edge of one of these dangerous places, and the next swept a hundred yards away by a tremendous "boil." Sometimes one end of the canoe became the bow, and at other times the opposite end, but at length we reached a little sandy cove and landed in still water. We had run the "Little Dalles" without knowing it.

CHAPTER XVI.

On our way we landed on a bar in the river at its upper end, and as the Indians were getting a meal ready, I saw what I took to be a deer jump into the river several hundred feet above us. I called the Indian, and we pushed the canoe up the shallow water above the bar, the Indian telling me it was a bear and not a deer that we were after. The strong current swept the bear near to us and we kept close to and above him. I was in the bow and could have laid my hand on him at any moment, but I wished to save him for food, and waited until we came close to the river bank, when, placing my revolver close behind his ear, I shot him dead. He plunged his head under the water, and catching hold of one of his hind legs we landed him. We now ran on down to the head of the Upper Arrow Lake, and finding the mosquitoes very numerous we camped on a small sandy shoal and proceeded to dry and smoke the bear.

At the head of the lake, a short distance to the right of the mouth of the river, I saw a large wooden cross. Curiosity induced me to find its origin, and I afterwards learnt the following :— One of the Hudson Bay Company's boats was running the Columbia from "The Boat Encampment" to Colville. They were always accustomed to take out the cargoes and passengers, and drop the boats with a line over the bad rapid known as the "Dalle de Mort." A person in the boat, who did not know the river, accused the crew of cowardice, and seizing the steering oar, forced the boat into the rapid and swamped her, only one man ever being known to have escaped. After long wandering he reached Fort Colville in a half insane state, and from his ravings it was feared he had been guilty of cannibalism. The officer in charge sent up a boat, and the few bodies found were buried under the cross I saw. Hence the name of the rapid, "Dalle de Mort," or "Death Rapid."

end,
at I
ibove
allow
1 not
near
r and
ed to
bank,
dead.
ne of
) the
very
o dry

)f the
iosity
ie fol-
was
) Col-
argoes
ie bad
t, who
e, and
d and
:caped.
insane
ilty of
ie few
ee the

I could see nothing of the branch party I was in hopes of meeting, having sent it from Kamloops to try for a line from " Cherry Creek " to the head of the " Arrow Lakes." Returning up the river great difficulty was experienced in poling our canoe against the strong current, and we were at the same time nearly devoured by mosquitoes, as we had to keep close to the bank. We landed at a place that had evidently been much used for a camping ground in previous years, and found a very old blaze on a fir tree. In black figures as clear as on the day they were written, were the latitude and longitude, signed with the name of Mr. Thompson, astronomer and explorer for the Hudson Bay Company, with the date, A.D. 1828, I think. I have, unfortunately, lost my original note of this, but my latitude agreed with his ; our longitudes were slightly different. It was valuable information for me.

When we had nearly reached the point I intended to make the exploration back to the Shuswap Lake, to see if I could find a pass by the opening before described as having been seen from that lake. I camped, and the next day landed with the purpose of reaching the ridge of the mountain range, and following it to the boundary line to make certain that should there be a pass I might not miss it. At the little creek where we landed, I went through the woods, and on looking into the water below me, saw a number of salmon, and one big fellow with a stick through his body, behind the others. This I knew to be the end of a spear an Indian we met the previous evening had told me he had lost in spearing a salmon. I called Perry, who was a very powerful man, and he thought he could catch the salmon ; so he got into the creek, a short distance below the fish, and cautiously approached until he managed to make a grab at each projecting end of the stick. The salmon gave a jump, striking Perry on one arm, nearly broke it, knocked Perry down, and escaped.

We now ascended a very steep, thickly-timbered mountain side, and camped on it. The following day we reached an upper plateau and travelled through beautiful grassy glades, innumerable flowers, and most picturesque groves of fir trees, and camped at

the foot of a high peak.* This peak I ascended, and could see a
fine valley extending to the far-off Shuswap Lake, and a continuation
of it running westerly to the Columbia River, and also a valley
extending far to the southward   Was this the anxiously wished-
for pass ?   How much depended upon it ?   How would it affect
the future prospects of British Columbia and of Canada ?   These
and many other questions passed through my thoughts during that
almost sleepless night.   Before daylight, leaving my companions,
who could not understand my hurry, to follow after me, I was off
to the bottom of the valley, and on reaching the stream found the
water flowing westward and a low valley to the eastward.   I
blazed a small cedar tree and wrote upon it, " *This is the Pass for
the Overland Railway,*" and then pushed eastward to the Columbia
River, which we all reached on the following day.   We now
commenced our journey up to the depôt for supplies to enable us
to explore a valley which I saw, running far to the eastward into
the Selkirks, and in a direct line with the pass I had just discovered.   And though a pass through the Selkirk range was not
to be compared in importance with one through the Gold range—
for one could always follow the valley of the Columbia River from
the east end of the Eagle Pass, and reach any of the passes
through the Rocky Mountains south of the Yellowhead Pass—yet,
it was evident that by shortening the distance, such a pass would
add most materially to the commercial prosperity of our future
railway, provided excessive grades would not be required

* I wished to name this peak, or rather mountain, " Mount Moody," after
my old friend Colonel Richard Clement Moody, of the Royal Engineers ,
and now that the pass first seen from it has really turned out to be all that
I then anticipated, and the railway is now going through it, I trust in any
future maps it may be so named

e a
tion
lley
ied-
fect
nese
that
ons,
s off
the
, I
for
abia
now
e us
into
dis-
not
ge—
rom
asses
-yet,
ould
ture

after
ers ;
that
i any

CHAPTER XVII.

On reaching our depôt I organised for the explorations in the Selkirks, and was joined by my assistant-engineers, Mr. Ashdown Green, C.E., and Mr. James Turnbull, late of the Royal Engineers. Mr. Green had been exploring the mountains to the north of me, and Mr. Turnbull those to the south. I sent Mr. Green to explore the valley of Gold River, Mr. Turnbull the valley of the In-com-opolux at the north-east end of the Upper Arrow Lake, and went myself to the valley I had seen opposite the pass discovered from Shuswap Lake. I reached it with a good outfit and Indians, three of whom were Columbia-river Indians. We ran the "Little Dalles" in a terrific thunder and lightning storm, accompanied with hail, and having a large canoe this time, well and strongly manned, it was a splendid and exciting trip, the Indians singing and shouting in grand style, enjoying it I think as much as I did. We camped a short distance up the Ille-cille-waet River, and having given Mr. Turnbull his supplies and final instructions, we wished each other farewell, and I turned my steps eastward, bound for the heart of that rugged Selkirk range. We toiled through dense underbrush and forests, and I was taken so sick that I had to camp. Victor, one of the Columbia-river Indians, boiled some roots and gave me the water to drink, and I became quite well again. After a hard scramble we reached the point where the river branches, one valley turning to the northward, the other having a south-easterly course. My Indians had intimated to me they would not go beyond this point as the winter was close at hand, and that we could not then cross the range and reach the Kootanie River. All possible inducements in the shape of rewards were unavailing, and it was with deep regret that I had to give up the idea then. I managed to get them to go some distance up the northerly fork, but the snow coming on we

returned.   That *south-easterly* branch is now adopted by the
Canadian Pacific Railway.   From my experience I believe rich gold
quartz and argentiferous galena mines will be worked in this range.
We ourselves found fair prospects of gold, and some very rich argentiferous galena.   On our journey we killed several porcupines,
which we ate with relish.   They are stupid animals, and we knocked
them on the head with sticks : we also killed some willow grouse
The Indian dog, "Minne-cox," was a great hunter, and would
come several times a day to me to pull out the porcupine quills
he managed to get in his mouth and lips.   When he got a
grouse on a tree he would watch me carefully until I fired, and
then it was a race to get the grouse first—if he were ahead I
never saw the grouse again.   It was amusing to see this dog
cache (hide away safely) any surplus food he did not need, to be
used on some future day.   On the morning of our proposed return
I aroused one of the Indians, Delina by name, just as the day was
breaking, and he having rubbed his eyes, caught my arm, and in
a mysterious manner and half-whisper, said : "I see bear; Hyas
bear," the latter meaning a big or grizzly bear.   I thought the
bear was close on us in the brush, but the Indian pointed him
out on a "bench" by the side of a mountain torrent, about one-
third of a mile away.   Perry, myself, Victor, and Delina at once
started to meet him.   Perry was armed with a small pea rifle,
Victor with a flint rock-B. gun, Delina with a little pea rifle, and
I with a revolver.   It was arranged that Perry and Victor should
make through the brush a short distance above the stream, and
I and Delina straight for the bear, but we were to wait until they
fired.   Delina and I came close up to the bench upon which the
bear was tearing up roots, and he evidently smelt something, for
he sat on his haunches and sniffed the air in all directions.   In
a few moments the report of a gun was heard, when Delina,
climbing up the rock, saw the bear also climbing up a rock slide
just above us.   Another shot was fired by one of the others, and
down came the bear as we stood on the edge of the rock.   He
immediately turned upon us and stood upon his hind legs ; then
we saw how enormous a brute he was, apparently ten feet high.

the
gold
nge.
1 ar-
ines,
cked
ouse
ould
quills
ot a
, and
ad I
dog
to be
eturn
y was
nd in
Hyas
; the
l him
; one-
once
, rifle,
e, and
hould
1, and
l they
h the
g, for
. In
elina,
slide
, and
He
then
high.

Delina's gun snapped, and he called out, "Hyah clattawa" (Quick—clear out, or run), and we both jumped over the edge of the precipice, some 15 or 18 feet, expecting the bear would be on the top of us. In the meantime the others had joined us, and we rose, when Victor made a shot that struck the bear's backbone and paralyzed his hind legs, and we all ignominiously attacked him. He made frantic efforts to get at us by drawing himself along with his paws, but he was too much disabled. I fired the contents of my revolver at his head, only distant five or six feet, but found not a single one cut through his enormous skull; at last Perry got a bullet through his heart, and he was dead. He was very fat, and the Indians skinned him, secured all the choice pieces and his head, and returned to camp, where they had such a gorge that I could not get them away that day. They stuck his head on a pole, decorating it with such white and red cotton rags as they could collect from their tattered clothing telling me that if they did not do so they would have no luck. Providing ourselves with some of the choice meat, we were ready for a start next morning. We had left the camp but a short distance in the morning, Victor and myself being last, when I heard a peculiar sound behind us. Victor was busy taking his gun out of the blanket covering, but did not move or take his pack off, and motioned me to remain still; presently I saw a magnificent Cariboo running straight towards us, but when some forty feet distant he went on one side with a beautiful long lope, and a shot from Victor's gun brought him to the ground. He was a very beautiful animal and in good condition. I was afraid of a repetition of the bear feast, but the Indians quietly cut off the best pieces, broke his legs to get the marrow, which they ate raw, and I then got them off. We only encountered another grizzly which I walked upon, and was within twenty feet before I saw him; he was an enormous animal. We had a good look at each other, and I made off in one direction and he in another; if I had had my rifle with me a better opportunity for a good shot could not have been had. We duly reached our canoe and returned to our depôt and thence to Seymour, discharging my Columbia-river Indians at the depôt. After arriving at Seymour I at once left in a canoe to go over the westerly portion of the pass I had discovered, but had hardly started when three miners followed, bringing me instructions to act as Gold Commissioner, and grant licences, &c. This necessitated my returning to the Columbia River, but not until I had completed the exploration of the pass as far as the tree I had formerly blazed. I then returned, in very cold weather, to the Columbia River, performed the necessary duties and made my way to Kamloops, where I had a cordial welcome, and returned to New Westminster. On my way down the Shuswap River I was detained a short time arranging with the Indians in regard to their reserves, which I accomplished satisfactorily, and then visited Adam's Lake. Here I made the acquaintance of Adam and Eve, an Indian and his wife, and went a short distance up the lake, thus closing the field work for that year.

CHAPTER XVIII.

A.D. 1866.—The office work for the season being completed, I applied for leave of absence for a short time, but had hardly got away when I was recalled. A deputation had waited on the Governor to have various work done on the Columbia River section of the country, and the miners, merchants, and others were greatly excited over the gold discoveries made the previous autumn, so that I was soon off once more to open trails and prosecute explorations. I reached the lower end of the great Shuswap Lake, where I met two old friends, Captain Moffatt and Mr. Joseph McKay, of the Hudson Bay Company. Captain Moffatt was engaged in building the steamer *Marten*, to run from Savona's Ferry, the westerly end of Kamloops Lake, to Seymour and other points on the Shuswap Lakes and rivers, and Mr. McKay had just returned from Seymour. I learnt from Mr. McKay that ice was still on the great Shuswap Lake, except in places along the shore. Miners and traders were crowding up, so I hired a large log canoe and started the following day, dragging the canoe over the ice where we could not find open water. At Seymour I found houses being rapidly built and everything in an excited state, all being most anxious to get to the mines. I went over to the Columbia River and found the snow very deep for eight miles over the summit plateau. I laid out and commenced a trail from La Porte, the head of steamboat navigation, above the 49th parallel, and a short distance below the " Dalle de Mort." The steamer " 49 " arrived on her first trip from Colville at this time. I now returned to the " Summit," and put a large force of men to cut a passage for pack animals through the deep snow. Many of the men suffered from snow blindness, but I got the trails opened and ran down with two of my Indians and a foreman to Fort Shepherd. Here I remained a day, when having got a party together and supplies, &c., &c., for my foreman to put the trail to

E

Wild Horse creek in order, I went to Wild Horse creek itself, and after staying a day went on, following the valley of the Kootanie, to the point where it turns into the Rocky Mountains, when fording the river and still following this peculiar great valley along the western base of the Rocky Mountains, came to the Columbia Lake, about one and a quarter mile distant from the crossing of the Kootanie River. The Columbia Lake is the source of the great river of that name, which has a length of about twelve hundred miles, and flows nearly north to the "Boat Encampment" in lat. 52° 7′ N., and then takes a sudden bend and runs nearly south through the Arrow Lakes into the territory of the United States ; hence the Selkirk range of mountains, which are within this bend of the river, derived the name by which it was generally known amongst the early prospectors and others, viz., "The Big Bend." The Selkirk range does not extend north of the Boat Encampment, but the Gold and Rocky Mountain ranges come nearly together at this point, being divided by the valley of the Canoe river, which has its source in the mountains not far from Tête Jaune Cache, on the Fraser River. This cache is the westerly end of the pass of the same name, now more generally known as the "Yellow-head Pass." I now followed the east shore of the Columbia Lake, which is some eight miles in length, and the valley of the Columbia through a very pretty country, in places like parks, with the Rocky Mountains towering above me on the right, and my old acquaintances, the Selkirks, covered with dense green forests, on the left. At a short distance below the Columbia Lake I suddenly rode into a large camp of the Kootanie Indians, and I was as much surprised as they were. They had a large number of horses, some of which they had stolen from the "Blackfeet," and as many of them were rather fine-looking animals, I presumed the Blackfeet had stolen them from some unfortunate whites. I camped close to them and had a general visit from men, women and children. I gave them a little tobacco and they returned me some dried meat, but whether it was bear, buffalo, or other meat, I could not tell—I only hoped it was not dog's flesh. Pushing on still through a similar country, we saw many piles of elk horns bleached quite white, indicating that those animals must have been very plentiful at some period in the past. I saw some very fine larch trees, and in the evening reached the end of the trail and the commencement of the thick woods. During the day I had been joined by two Indians and a very good-looking young squaw, the wife of one of the men. He was evidently very jealous of his spouse, and because of this she suffered a severe knock on the head. She managed to get me an old log canoe, and sending my horses back to the men working on the trail, we crossed the river, and at a short distance came to a little camp of Shuswap Indians, where I met their head man, " Kinbaskit." I now negociated with him for two little canoes made of the bark of the spruce, and for his assistance to take me down the river. Kinbaskit was a very good Indian, and I found him always reliable. He knew the Columbia thoroughly, and proved himself most useful to me at that time as well as in after years, when I again visited that country during the time I was in the service of the Canadian Pacific Railway.

CHAPTER XIX.

I had to wait at camp, as an Indian Kinbaskit wished to take with him was down the river. I found there were at a creek below that point some bears who came at night for the salmon, which were there in great quantities at the time, and thereupon went down before dark with a gun to try and secure one. I squeezed myself into a dense grove of thorn bushes in a muddy bend of the stream and awaited their arrival. The night was cold, and at last I heard the bears feeding on the salmon, but it was so dark I could see nothing. The cold increased, and I thought I would retreat to my camp, but at every move I came across a few of the thorns, and I could not get out. Shivering in the mud until daylight I found a wretched amusement, and to return without even having a shot at a bear was most annoying. Our two canoes being ready we commenced our voyage, and nothing of very great importance took place. I sketched the river, took latitudes and estimated longitudes, looked into the westerly ends of the Kicking Horse and Howse Passes, and found they were favourably situated to connect with the Eagle Pass. We ran many rapids and portaged others, then came to a Lake which I named "Kinbaskit" Lake, much to the old chief's delight. From this lake to the "Boat Encampment" the water was very bad indeed, the distance being about twenty-two miles. We camped at that old landing of the Hudson Bay Company's boats, where the Canoe and the Wood or Portage Rivers empty their waters into the Columbia. A very sad story is connected with the "Boat Encampment." Many years ago, when a brigade was on its way from Colville, among the passengers by the boats were the present Mrs. Captain H. S. Donaldson, of Winnipeg, Manitoba (then a child), and her mother. Some time after the brigade of horses had left on their way through the Athabasca Pass, the old lady was missed.

A search was made for her, but from that time not the slightest trace of her could be found. We now ran on down to the mouth of Gold creek (Wilson's landing), portaged the " Dalle de Mort," and then on as far as Kerby's landing, where I met Mr. Arthur Birch, the Colonial Secretary, and Captain H. M. Ball, one of the Gold Commissioners. I spent the night at their camp, and in the morning they left for New Westminster, and I returned to French creek. At one place, not far from the " Dalle de Mort," seeing an old hut I landed to find out what it was. As my Indians did not like to land I asked the reason why, and one of them told me that several years before a Columbia-river Indian, his wife and two children were staying in the hut. The Indian went in his canoe to visit his traps, but night came on, the woman watching for her husband's return. At last she heard the dip of his paddle in the water, and saw him step carefully out of his canoe at the usual landing-place and begin to unload his canoe, when she laid down again in her blankets. After a time, surprised at his not coming in, she got up, but could see no signs of the Indian or canoe, and went to the landing-place to examine the newly-fallen snow to see, as she expected, his footsteps, but was dreadfully frightened to find there were not any marks. A day or two afterwards two Indians of her tribe came and told her they had found her husband's broken canoe at the foot of a bad rapid, but could find no trace of him. His body never was found, and the wrecked canoe told the poor woman the mournful tale. The Indians believing the hut to be haunted by the spirit of the drowned Indian, do not like to go to it.

CHAPTER XX.

I remained a few days at French creek, winding up the season' business, and paid off my Indi ns from the Upper Columbia. I had promised them some money, a suit of clothes each, and as many provisions as they could pack. The morning after my arrival I went into a store and purchased a box of sardines for breakfast, out of which I ate a few and left the rest for the Indians, who appeared to enjoy them very much. After breakfast I took them into a store, got them clothes and some tobacco, and asked them what they would have for provisions. They promptly answered, "Teuass pish" (little fish), meaning sardines. I told them they would starve on them, but they were bound to have the fish with "hiyon grease" (plenty of grease), and nothing but the fish, so I loaded them with as many as they could carry, and they departed over the mountains homeward bound, shaking hands with me, saying I was a "Hyas closhe skookum Tyhee," that is, "a very good and powerful chief." A few days closed my business, and I left on my downward journey with Mr. White, the Clerk of the Chief Gold Commissioner. We got a dreadful drenching on our way to La Porte, and on arriving at Seymour were delighted to get on board the comfortable H.B. Company's steamer *Marten*, and enjoy an evening with my old friend Captain Moffatt, and some excellent English porter, &c., &c. We had a very pleasant run to Kamloops, where I stayed over-night at the fort, and then went on to New Westminster, where I prepared my maps, reports, &c., and at the end of the year left the service and went to San Francisco, leaving all my old friends with much regret.

son'
i. I
d as
rival
cfast,
who
them
them
ered,
they
with
, so I
arted
me,
very
and I
of the
n our
ted to
n, and
some
run to
ent on
, &c.,
San

CHAPTER XXI.

A.D. 1868-9.—I found San Francisco greatly changed since I left it ten years ago, so much so indeed that I did not know much of it. After a short stay I went up over a portion of the Central Pacific Railway, then in course of construction over the Sierra Nevada Mountains, and visited Grass Valley, &c. I had the opportunity of meeting one of the owners of the "Eureka Mine," which is a remarkably rich quartz gold mine, and has paid enormous dividends. I spent some months in San Francisco, visiting many of the neighbouring towns, where the scenery is in places very beautiful. There is a good drive from San Francisco to the Cliff House. The latter is well situated, affording a fine view over the adjoining portion of the Pacific Ocean and of the "Seal Rocks," which are a short distance from and a good many feet below its level. The rocks were covered with enormous seals, and it was rather amusing to watch them. I found the rainy or winter season the most pleasant, as in the summer the strong sea breeze that blows during a great portion of the day causes the dust to be annoying, but the nights are cool and enjoyable. I remained in San Francisco until the "White Pine" excitement took place, and then with many others went to the interior. Bad weather and such like induced me to remain in Elko, where I did a most profitable business for a short time, surveying and painting signs. Reports of finds of rich silver in the Red Hills on the Awyhee River induced about eighty of us to go there. None of us knew the exact road, and in such a great hurry were we to reach our destination that we travelled at night, got scattered in small parties, and indeed lost our way. We had a little adventure : as some of us were riding along a high mountain side we saw a large bear go into a grove of cottonwood trees in the bottom of the valley below us. An American miner and myself, leaving our horses with the rest of the party, crept down to get a shot at him. We had once a glimpse of the animal but missed him   Some of the party then began firing into the grove of trees, which were not large and we were in danger of being shot, many bullets coming close to us. To stop this we fired back, taking care that our bullets went very close while not hitting them, and thus the bear got away.   Travelling through an enormous army of locusts for a whole day, we arrived at a pretty flat on the Awyhee River, and close to the "Argenta silver mine," which had caused the excitement. We formed a mining district, appointed a recorder, and prospected and took up claims. I returned to Elko and obtained a large supply of provisions and mining tools, which were provided by a gentleman who wished to join me in mining. We returned and I laid out a city for the original discoverers, which took me three days. For this I was handsomely paid and given two good lots as a bonus. Then for a time I did a most remunerative business as mining engineer, and at the same time sunk several prospecting shafts on our mines in this and two adjoining districts   A very severe winter came on and we were nearly starved out, communication being cut off by the deep snow. Many miners were without provisions, and several of my acquaintances used to congregate at my shanty to get one "square" meal a day. At last my supplies ran low, so one day I thought I would go to a pond on the river, where I had caught trout, and try an experiment   I "fixed" up a giant cartridge in such a way that it would explode under water, and made a hole in the ice; exploding the cartridge I ran below the pond, where there was a small rapid and no ice, when in a short time the stunned fish began to float down and I secured a good bag full. A friend of mine, Judge ———, was at that time badly off for provisions, but he had some good whisky and white German wine, so I told him if he would provide a bottle of each I would provide a capital supper ; the offer was accepted, and we passed a pleasant evening. He was anxious to know how I obtained the fish, and in a moment of weakness I told him. The following morning, on leaving my cabin, I was surprised to see a notice on my door, which was an extract from some law, which informed me that the killing of fish in the manner adopted by me was a serious offence, and certainly not in accordance with the law. At my subsequent fish dinners I was careful not to invite acquaintances.

below
h the
e had .
party
large
g close
bullets
ar got
for a
r, and
excite-
r, and
tained
ovided
urned
ok me
good
rative
everal
ining
nearly
snow.
f my
one
one
had
giant
, and
v the
short
good
ndly
rman
vould
assed
ained

CHAPTER XXII.

Making a trip to "Bonno" to see about some of my mines, I laid out a "city" in a pretty valley below the principal ridges, and stayed to get some shafts sunk and tunnels driven. The snow came on, and the few that had remained were short of provisions. One woman was in the camp, and we had nothing for it but to get out or starve A very fine fellow, who had two oxen, said he would make a "pung," a sort of a sled with the shafts and runners in the same piece of wood , I to provide the horse, of which I had three on the mountain, and take the woman out, and he going ahead with the oxen to break the trail He left at daylight, and I went after the horses, but could not find them, and after a hard trip through the snow returned at night On the next morning I resumed my search, which was successful, and in the afternoon I started with one man and the woman The snow was drifting, and when the darkness came on we could get no further, so I abandoned the sled, and, placing the woman on the horse, led it back to our cabin, which we reached after a dreadful trip, in which the poor woman suffered very much The storm did not abate for a day or two. We were in a state almost of starvation, and concluded to make some "Norwegian snow-shoes." These snow-shoes are made about eight or ten feet in length, and four or five inches in width ; they are quite thin and light, and on flat ground or down hill, glide along easily and swftly. The whole party having equipped themselves with snow-shoes, and a heavy pair having been made into a sled with a seat for the woman, we left on one fine morning, and progressed very well until we came to a long descent. An accident happened to the man who was assisting me with the sled, in which it ran down the declivity, leaving the poor woman in the snow at the bottom, unhurt, and breaking the sled. It was now apparent that the sled

was a failure, and two of the men agreed to help the woman along,
I giving her my snow-shoes, and taking the ones used for the
runners of the sled. They went on, and I remained to rig the
runners into snow-shoes, which after a time I did, but in a very
imperfect manner, not having the proper appliances. Following
their tracks, with the cord I had to use to fasten my feet to the
shoes cutting my feet, I had a long, painful, and dreary walk, and
just as night was coming on overtook the party high up on the
sloping mountain. All were weary and tired; the woman sat
down and cried with fatigue. There was was no shelter, and
nothing but the most dreary of dreary prospects ahead. We
knew there was a wayside tent-house on the stage road, but as
we had, on the recommendation of one of the party who said he
knew all about the country, taken a short cut, none of us knew
exactly where we were, and our guide, the most confused of the
party, was not complimented. A plucky fellow, a Norwegian,
assisted me to pull the woman along, and that dreary walk we
shall never forget. Hour after hour passed. At length I proposed they should stop, and I go ahead to look for sign of
house or shelter of any kind, the rest of the party to remain
and answer my pistol shots should I not be able to find them.
I had not gone far when I saw a distant light in the valley
below us, and returned with the welcome news. We all slid
down the mountain side into the valley, along which we proceeded on tolerably flat ground. I was obliged, at last, to
follow instead of lead, my feet being so sore and feeling quite
used up. The house was not far off and the others reached it, but
I floundered into a deep ravine, and throwing off my hateful snow-
shoes crawled into the place so thoroughly worn out that I lay
down on a pile of wood and slept soundly until the morning.

CHAPTER XXIII.

In the morning we were surprised to find one of our party missing, and strange to say it was the man who had essayed to guide us. Two of the party and I started back to find him. After travelling about two-thirds of the distance back to the mining camp, we espied a black object sitting on the snow, and there found the unfortunate fellow sitting on his snow-shoes in a half-dazed state, his feet being slightly frozen. He had completely lost himself. When we slid down the mountain on the previous night, he was behind, the night was dark, and he not knowing where we were, got turned round, and was actually retracing his steps to the place whence we started. The rest of the ensuing winter of 1869-70 was passed in rather a monotonous manner, principally occupied in prospecting our mines. A large gambling saloon had been built close to my shanty, and occasional rows and shooting scrapes occurred. Several bullets struck my shanty, which was by no means bullet-proof, so that when I heard a row for safety I got out of my bunk and lay on the floor. This was a great nuisance, and getting a large square log I put it alongside my bed, forming a bullet-proof battery, behind which I could sleep in peace. At the near approach of the following winter we found the mines were a complete failure. We had expended a very large amount of money, and could not get in a dollar that was due to us, so abandoning or giving away all our remaining outfit we made for the railway, my friend securing a free pass and I selling my horse, saddle, and bridle to pay my fare, to find on reaching San Francisco only five dollars in my pocket. I took up my quarters at a good hotel, determined to have one good night's rest and a substantial breakfast, and then strolled down Montgomery street to California street, wondering what next to do. As I was standing there in the forenoon, the Mining Board of Brokers adjourned, and I met one of those with whom I had successfully dabbled, in a small way, in stocks. He wished me to take a venture in some stock he had just purchased and felt certain it would take a rise. I told him I would take some so that the margin to be put up should not exceed seven hundred dollars, and I would meet him when the afternoon Board closed, but he was to be certain to sell should the stock go up. I hurried off to see a very old friend who at that time was very well off, and requested the loan of a cheque for a few months for the amount, which he gave me. I then returned, waiting anxiously for the closing of the Board, when I met my friend, who told me he had been most successful, the stock having gone up, and he there and then paid me seven hundred and twenty dollars as my share of the profits, I had not thus to use my borrowed cheque, but returned it to my friend that evening with many thanks, and found myself comparatively rich for a short time.

Not long afterwards, in the early part of 1871, the Utah mining excitement broke out, and I met a Scotch assayer whom I had known in Nevada, and who had just returned from Utah. He was greatly excited about the new silver and lead mines, and recommended me to go up at once. I found my old mining partner and we both started for Utah. On arrival at Salt Lake City I called on the Mormon Prophet, "Brigham Young," from whom I acquired much valuable information and civility, as I also did from other Mormons during my stay in that territory. I prospected for some time, until I received a telegram from Ottawa informing me that the Canadian Pacific Railway was to be commenced, and requesting me to leave for Ottawa at once. The next morning, giving my companions my outfit and mining interests, I went to Salt Lake City and thence to Ottawa, where I saw my old friend of early days, Mr. Sandford Fleming, and Sir John A. Macdonald (at that time Premier of Canada), and gave them full information as to the feasibility of a line for a railway through that country, and which is the one now adopted. After a short stay at Ottawa, having been appointed District

Engineer of the country between Shushwap Lake and the easterly foot hills of the Rocky Mountains, I, with a few other engineers, &c., returned to the Pacific Coast, and on reaching Victoria, Vancouver Island, organised our parties and landed the first of them on the mainland on the day which saw British Columbia become a portion of the Dominion of Canada, viz., Dominion Day. I at once called upon my old friend Sir James Douglas, from whom I received a hearty greeting.

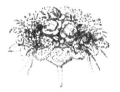

rly
rs,
ia,
of
bia
ion
las.

CHAPTER XXIV.

Having partly organised our parties at Victoria, and purchased supplies, we sailed for New Westminster, and thence up the Fraser River. I landed with party S at Fort Hope, the others going on to Yale. There I found the men who had engaged themselves as packers, on account of the higher pay, but they knew little or nothing about packing, and had to be degraded to the ranks, while others were sent for. This caused a little delay, but the party got off with a fully-equipped pack train of mules and a few horses, bound for Wild Horse creek before described, as a branch of the Kootani River. I followed the others, purchased and forwarded all the provisions I could get at Yale, and, on my way to Kamloops, purchased beef, cattle, and pack-animals for the different parties. We all met at Savona's Ferry, and putting party T with some supplies on board a batean, they went on to Kamloops, to which place I also travelled in a small log canoe in company with Mr. A. R. C. Selwyn, Director of the Geological Survey of Canada. At Kamloops we were very busy getting the parties equipped for the survey of the North Thompson River and Yellowhead Pass, which was Mr. Roderic McLennan's district; and that by the South Thompson, or Shuswap River and Lakes, the Eagle Pass in the Gold range, and the passes in the Selkirk and Rocky Mountains, which embraced my district. On the 15th of August I left for Fort Colville, following the trail *viâ* Okanagan Lake, Osooyoos Lake, and Fort Colville, taking one of my assistants and three Indians. I had purchased a fine, though very wild and vicious horse, which we led the first day, but he got away, and we had a long chase to capture him. The following day I rode him, but had proceeded only half a mile, when, as he was going along very quietly, he suddenly threw me in the most incomprehensible manner, and we had a long and useless chase, but could not catch him, and the horse, saddle, bridle, &c., I never saw again. I now went on to the Roman Catholic Mission, where I stopped over-night, and spent a very pleasant evening with the priest, Father ——— (I have forgotten his name), and thence to Osooyoos Lake, where I met Mr. Lowe, from whom I purchased two horses, and stayed an evening at his house, meeting there the United States Customs' Officer from Fort Colville. The next day I went on to Rock creek, where we stayed over-night. It was on the way to this point that my surveys were nearly stopped for good. I happened as I was moving on to tread on a rattlesnake, which kept striking at my leg with his fangs, but fortunately I had heavy riding boots on, and a sufficient length of his body not being free, he could not reach above the leather ; and so I escaped unharmed, which it is almost needless to say he did not.

CHAPTER XXV.

Leaving my Indians and pack-animals to follow, I made a rapid trip to Old Fort Colville, wishing to get there and purchase supplies, &c., before the object of my trip was known, as supplies were scarce. I arrived in the evening, and bought up all available supplies, and chartered the steamer "49," which was laid up to make a trip to "The Eddy," which is the easterly end of Eagle Pass, and went on about fourteen miles to the American garrison at New Fort Colville, where at the adjoining village I purchased all supplies in the place. This was fortunate, for next day prices went up 30 per cent. I was very kindly entertained by the army officers at the Fort, where I spent the night, and the next day pursued my journey eastward. The country I passed through from Kamloops to Colville is a very pretty one, nearly the whole distance being diversified with beautiful rivers, streams, lakes, prairies, and mountains. There are some good and picturesque farms at and in the vicinity of the north end of Okanagan Lake, those of Colonel Houghton, Deputy Adjutant-General of Manitoba, and the Messrs. Vernon being delightfully situated. The Mission is also an attractive place, and there is a good deal of fair agricultural land about it. I now followed the pretty agricultural valley of the Colville River, where there are many farms, and journeying on through Idaho territory, recrossed the boundary line, and came on the trail from Fort Shepherd to Wild Horse creek, the country from the boundary line being generally thickly timbered, rocky, and mountainous.

I overtook my party S a short distance west of the pretty prairie, known as "Joseph's Prairie," and thence by the same trail I have before described to Wild Horse creek. Here I arrived on September 11th, and taking up my quarters in the abandoned H. B. station, a short distance below the mining camp,

F

went on to the village where I met Gold Commissioner J. C. Haynes and the late Mrs. Haynes, finding in both very old acquaintances, whom I had known in the early Crown Colony days. An attempt was here made to force me to increase the pay of the men—a movement instigated by one dissatisfied man, whom I dismissed on the spot, with the assurance he should never do another day's work for me. The others, who had all engaged with me for two years, then withdrew. We now went on to the "Boat Landing," so named from its being the point where our boats and canoes took the cargoes down the river, the pack-animals proceeding by land through the thickly timbered flats bordering the Columbia River. Some of the animals not arriving, I went back a short distance, expecting to be away until the following day, but fortunately returned that evening, when it appeared some one or two of my employés had made improper overtures to some of the squaws accompanying Indians whom I proposed to work in the canoes and boats. The Indians wished to leave, which was a serious matter, so to put an end to such occurrences, I dismissed the men on the spot, and gave notice that any similar conduct by men in my employ would meet with like treatment, and also loss of pay. It might be perhaps regarded as a rather arbitrary proceeding on my part, but it was unquestionably most advantageous for the success and general welfare of the expedition. The boats and canoes being loaded, we ran on down with the party and supplies to a point a short distance above the mouth of the "Blacberry River," which flows through the westerly slope of the Howse pass. Here we formed our depôt, intending it to be the main depôt on the Columbia river *for the surveys I proposed making through the Howse and Kicking Horse Passes; along the valley of the Columbia River, around the "Big Bend," from Kicking Horse to Eagle Pass, and across the Selkirk range by the valley of the Ille-cille-waet River and its south-easterly branch,* which latter and proposed part I should make after the completion of the survey through the Eagle Pass. On the 2nd of October, I gave orders to open a trail and make a preliminary survey through the Howse Pass, and set the party at this work, going on with Indians and horses through the woods by this pass, with the intention of reaching the easterly end of the Kootani Plain on the North Saskatchewan River. This spot is close to, but on the opposite bank of the river, from Mount Murchieson, so named by Dr. Hector, when he was with the expedition sent out in the years 1857-8-9 by the Imperial Government under the command of Captain Palliser. I found such portions of the country as had been traversed by them, and visited by me, most accurately and clearly described, and indeed found a copy of their reports of the greatest value. On leaving the valley of the Blaeberry River, and emerging through the "Blaeberry Nick" into the head waters of the North Saskatchewan, I was enchanted with the grand scenery. In bold relief before me, stood Mount Forbes with its towering form partly covered with grassy slopes, partly with thick green timber, with perpetual snow above, and magnificent glaciers like transparent blue grass in the bright sunshine. Reaching the main stream we rode over open gravel flats which are covered at high water, and followed them to some low partially wooded sand hills opposite the stream, coming from the north from Glacier Lake, where we camped. A beautiful clear moonlight followed, and lighting my pipe, I strolled along enjoying the magnificent scenery until I came to a point of a thick grove of fir-trees that jutted out on the gravel flats. Resting myself against a tree, my two little dogs went to sleep at my feet, when suddenly we were startled by the dismal cry of a panther close to us, which caused a precipitate retreat to the camp. The cry of a panther much resembles that of a child, they grow to a large size, are cowardly animals, and not to be much feared.

CHAPTER XXVI.

We journeyed on for some distance, following the right bank of the river, on a good well-beaten trail, seeing some old buffalo skulls and bones, and the remains of a recently killed elk, and camped near the westerly end of the "Kootami Plain" in a thick grove of black pine trees, not of any great size.   The following morning we passed through "Kootami" Plain, and sought in every direction for traces of my brother Frank's party, who were to extend their explorations from the east and connect with mine. We forded the river, and finding no traces of them re-crossed and camped.   The Kootami Plain is a beautiful spot, having open prairies and clumps of trees, to the beauty of which the surrounding mountains add greatly.   I learnt from Dr. Hector's Journal, that its name originated from the Kootami Indians coming from the west to trade with the Indians on the east side of the Rocky Mountains, and it was a place very much famed amongst Indian hunters for the great quantity of game to be found there, but which had been killed many years ago by a disease (and no doubt by the Indians after the introduction of firearms.—W. M.).   I now returned and met the party a short distance down the valley of the Blacberry River, at a place which we called "Three Creek Flats," as three creeks form a junction there.   The weather now grew colder and it began to snow.   I found the levels taken by me with a very good aneroid barometer corrected with a "boiling point thermometer," both of which were of the very best make, correspond closely with those taken by the leveller of the party, one making the difference in height, from a common point on the Columbia River to another on the "Flat," 1,607 feet, and the other 1,610 feet.   In the morning we all went up, through the snow, to try and run the line down from a point near the "summit," but the snow fell so heavily that we could make no progress, and returned to our camp after dark, thoroughly drenched, and feeling very miserable. The next morning we retreated a short distance further down, in hopes of being able to get the survey from that point, but the snow fell thicker than ever, and I gave orders to retreat to the depôt. Here we were busily occupied in plotting the results of our surveys, and in the erection of the buildings in which the men were to winter. I set some men at work building boats for the next summer's work, and having everything in satisfactory shape on the 4th of December, bid adieu to party S, and left with my Indians to cross the Selkirk range, visit party T in the Gold range, and make my way by the Eagle Pass, &c., to Victoria, as I then expected to go on to Ottawa.

CHAPTER XXVII.

We were all provided with good snow-shoes, without which it would be impossible to travel in these mountains in winter, except at a snail's pace, the snow being deep and soft. The journey down the Columbia River was monotonous, occasionally enlivened by some member of the party falling through the ice, to be fished out by the others. At length we came to the point where I decided to cross the Selkirks, and strike the head waters of the Gold River. I wished to see if a pass might not be obtained here, and a survey of it be necessary as well as that I had already decided to make by the Ile-cille-waet River, and its south-easterly branch. We had fearful work ascending the narrow and rugged valley of the stream we followed owing to the deep, soft snow, dense timber and underbrush, but at length we reached a high narrow pass through which we travelled. When we began to descend the western slope of the mountains we crossed a small lake, with a glacier on its north side, which was not far above our level, and at a short distance we descended a long and very steep portion of the mountain side, and came upon Gold River. This we followed, passing through a dense forest of magnificent trees of the usual description met with in these mountains, such as will doubtless be of great value in future for the supply of the prairie country to the eastward of the Rocky Mountains, provided that civilization does not bring with it destructive bush fires. Wending our way through the large forest trees, we came in the early part of an evening on some fresh snow-shoe tracks leading over a high projecting part of the mountain to the north of us. Along these tracks we descended into the valley of French creek, to find ourselves in the nearly deserted mining town, where, though I had not visited it since 1866, I met old acquaintances in the miners. We were gratified in obtaining a good supper in the only store in the place, and, discussing a few glasses of excellent rum and water, we slept soundly on the floor. Next day we remained on the "Creek" to recruit. I visited the miners' shanties, and also Mr. Vowel, the resident Gold Commissioner, and invited all hands to spend the evening with me, when I obtained much information about the mining in that part of the country since I was last there. Bidding adieu to my friends, I went on the following day only five miles to the deserted mining town of McCulloch's Creek, and slept in an old shanty, the weather being excessively cold. The next day, after a fatiguing walk we reached the old steamboat landing, "La Porte," a short distance below "Dalle de Mort," and found a solitary old man—Mr. Nichol—in whose cabin we slept. On the two following days we travelled partly by ice and partly by land against a strong and excessively cold wind, and reached the "Big Eddy," where we found party T in their winter house engaged in completing the plans, &c., of the line surveyed through the Eagle Pass. Here we stayed a short time to complete the plans, and here Christmas-day also was passed in a pleasant manner. Several of the party were good musicians and singers, and having brought a fiddle, flute, and accordion with them, our evenings were very merry. Once more I resumed my way and examined the line located. The travelling was bad, as the snow was soft and deep, and underbrush dense and covered with much snow, which fell off on our heads and at times got down our necks, in a way far from pleasant. The 1st of the new year was a most unpleasant day, and we all succeeded in having a bath or two in the river, as the ice was not strong. The weather continued remarkably warm after we left the Columbia valley. We now reached the Great Shuswap Lake, and crossed the narrows at the mouth of Eagle creek, and followed the south shore of the Salmon River arm for some distance, when I tried to cross to the north side to examine a low depression that appeared to connect this arm with the more northerly and almost parallel one, out of which the Shuswap River flows. I was ahead of the party, and managing to fall through the ice, was nearly drowned, the rottenness of the ice and absence of assistance rendering it a difficult task to get out. We camped, and on the next day finding open water opposite the depression above-mentioned, tied some logs together and rafted ourselves across. We then examined this valley on the following day, and found through it a feasible line for the railway. I gave no name to this little pass, as I could not find out the Indian name for it at that time. It undoubtedly has such a name, and I would suggest that it should retain it. On reaching the main Shuswap Lake we kicked off our snow-shoes, and I may here express my fervent hope that necessity may never again compel me to have snow-shoes on my feet, especially in such a country as we passed through on this long and arduous trip. After an easy journey I reached Kamloops, and once more took up my quarters in old and hospitable Fort Kamloops, with my esteemed friend Mr. John Tait. We now proceeded partly on foot, and partly by other modes of conveyance, to New Westminster, and thence to Victoria by steamer. As soon as I reached the telegraph line I was in a position to telegraph to Mr. Fleming, which I did, that a railway line *via* the Eagle Pass and the Columbia River and its tributary country, was practicable; and after many years since elapsed, in the exploratory surveys of many other lines, it is very gratifying indeed to see mine is the one finally adopted for the Canadian Pacific Railway.

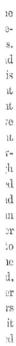

SAR AT CHEWING RIVER, NEAR THE ELBOW. STEAM DRILL AT WORK NEAR THE MAIN LINE OF THE CANADIAN PACIFIC RAILWAY.

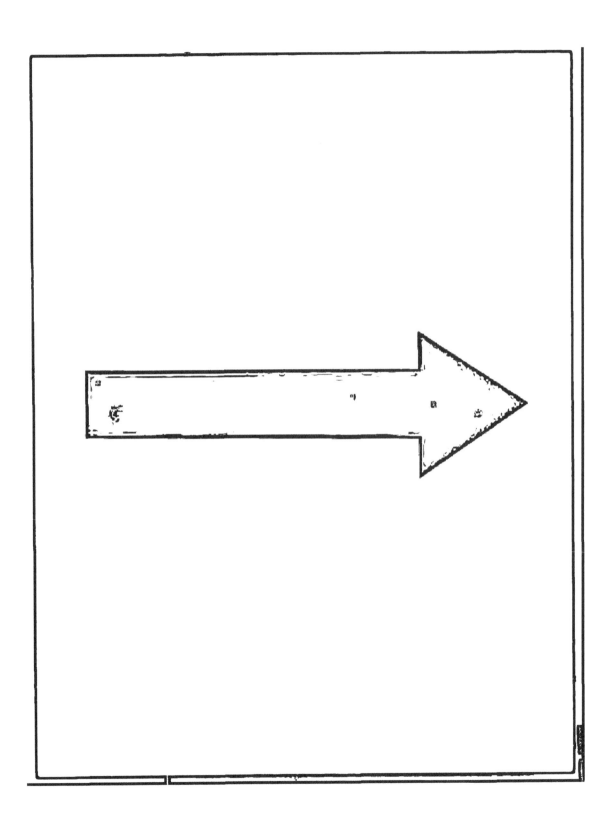

**IMAGE EVALUATION
TEST TARGET (MT-3)**

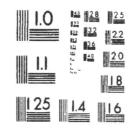

6"

Photographic
Sciences
Corporation

23 WEST MAIN STREET
WEBSTER, N Y 14580
(716) 872 4503

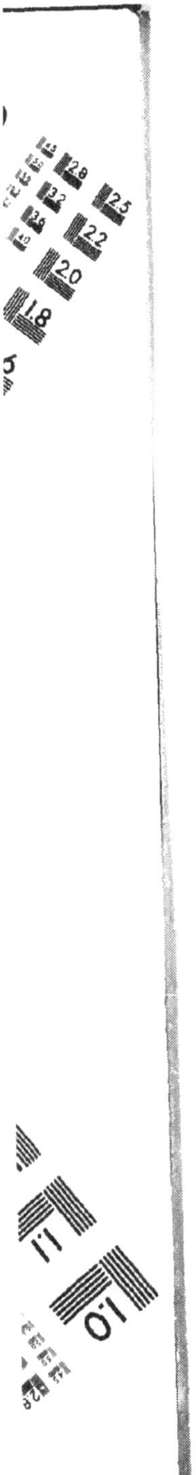

2.8
2.5
3.2
2.2
3.6
2.0
1.8
1.1
1.0

CHAPTER XXVIII.

The length of time it had taken in getting through all the mountain ranges left insufficient time for me to go to Ottawa, as preparations for the next season's work, on a much larger scale, were necessary to enable the Canadian Government to carry out the terms of the Confederation with British Columbia. I now felt quite certain that the railway would be built through the country I had examined, and every possible provision was made by me to complete the exploratory surveys and follow them with the location ones. Late in the evening of the day preceding the morning of my proposed departure for the interior, I was astounded to get a telegram instructing me to abandon all surveys in my district, and take charge of the surveys through the Yellowhead Pass. That a great mistake was being made could not but be apparent to me, and I so informed the Lieutenant-Governor, through whom the message came, but as a subordinate officer I had to obey orders, and went over to Portland, Oregon, to get out of the contracts, &c., I had entered into, and make such other arrangements as the new phase matters had taken might render necessary. We had a disagreeable journey from Olympia, Puget Sound, through the dense Oregonian forests, that extended on either side of that then most muddy road, breaking the hind wheels of a vehicle, miscalled a stage, and then enjoying a walk through the mud to Pomphrey's landing on the Cowlitz River. Here I met an old British Columbia friend, Mr. McCulloch, the discoverer of the creek of that name, in the " Big Bend " before referred to, and then in the employ of the Northern Pacific Railway, who treated me well, and on my leaving on the little steamer *Winat*, presented me with two bottles of excellent whisky. On our way down the Cowlitz River we succeeded in running a snag through the bottom of our rotten little craft, and in sinking her in shallow water, but as she was a light boat we pulled her on the side of the river, and stuffed a mattress and other things into the hole, and made our way to Montecello, where we connected the following morning with the steamer for the city of Portland, which is situated at the junction of the Willamette and Columbia Rivers. We arrived at Montecello on Sunday evening, and on reaching the solitary little hotel, we could find nobody about, but the supper, such as it was, was laid on the table ; we were all hungry, and rang a bell on the verandah, which had the effect of bringing a man in a very bad humour on the scene. This gentleman proved to be a deacon of the church and proprietor of the hotel, but we managed to pacify him and secured our suppers and beds. Next day we arrived in Portland, and took up our quarters in the St. Charles Hotel, kept by a genial landlord, Mr. Jacobs, formerly of the St. Nicholas, Victoria. Portland is the highest point in the Columbia River reached by sea-going vessels, and was at that time a very busy and thriving city of about thirty thousand inhabitants.

I went up to Oregon city, a few miles from Portland, on the Willamette River, where there is fine water power, and where an expensive canal for river steamers was then in course of construction around the rapids. I met with much civility from the head-man of the Oregon Steam Navigation Company, and travelled in one of their fine steamers up to Walledu, where we landed and found a wretched village of miserable houses partially covered with drifted sand. Thence I travelled to Walla Walla with the Chief Engineer of a portion of the Northern Pacific Railway, and his amiable wife. Walla Walla was then a very little town built on a rather flat country, and during the Indian wars in former years had been a large military post. After a short stay here we went on over a tolerably good road to Colville, where I remained for a short time to make various arrangements, and then pushed on through Idaho, purchasing all the pack-animals engaged in freighting our supplies, on my way, so as not to be left at the mercy of the packers. When I reached the Columbia river at the "Boat Landing," on the 14th, and meeting the boats built in the preceding winter at the Columbia River depôt, I had them loaded, and ran down to that depôt, which I reached on June 15th, 1872, and met a portion of party S, the others being further down the river, then opening the trail along it by which I proposed to convey my party and supplies into the Yellowhead Pass. An amusing incident occurred here : when I was in Portland I had become possessed of some bottles of champagne, which I had packed in a bundle of my blankets, and forgot all about them; but on overhauling my package the bottles made their appearance in a good state of preservation, and some of my party pronounced it to be of a very good quality. That was probably the first champagne drank on the McGillvray branch of the Columbia.

CHAPTER XXIX.

Some of the party at the depôt had the scurvy, but not very badly; and ascertaining it was principally their own fault, I gave them a severe blowing up, and putting the stores, &c., into the boats abandoned this dreary spot, and ran on to the " Slate Cañon," where the water is bad and not fit for loaded boats to run with safety. From the upper end of the Slate Cañon there is a curious valley on the east side of the Columbia, and nearly parallel to it, which runs down to a considerable stream which I named Placid River, and through this valley we opened a good pack trail. My men were now all busily engaged opening this trail and boating down the supplies as fast as they arrived at the boat-landing. I went down the river in a small canoe with two Indians to pick out a line ahead. Arriving at Placid River, I selected the spot to ferry across ; when finding a short though deep quagmire beyond the river, I tried to find a better crossing, but without success. Hearing some swans, we drew our canoe into a small lake where they were, and that day we had a grand hunt. The swans could not rise off the water, as they had not as yet the new feathers on their wings fully grown, and with my Henry rifle it was good sport, I only firing at their long necks. We got several, and returning to Placid River camped and cooked part of a swan, which was coarse and tough, but tasted very well. We now walked through the woods, blazing a line for the trail, and the second day met the party, with whom I camped ; and as some of the men had behaved very badly to the Engineer-in-charge, I ordered them up to my camp at the Slate Cañon, where I dismissed them, and sent them back to Wild Horse creek. We found the country rough in the extreme for opening up a trail, the heavy growth and great quantity of fallen timber being the most serious cause of delay. I went ahead

with Kinbaskit and two Indians to Kinbaskit Lake, taking a
canoe with us, to pick out the most favourable line we could find.
One day I was much troubled how to get along the side of a
mountain south of the lake, and sent my canoe back, retaining
only one Indian.   We scrambled up the heavily timbered mountain side, and there I espied a cub on a large Douglas fir; we
then ran to the tree, and sure enough two cubs were climbing up
as fast as they could go. Vainly I tried to knock them down with a
small revolver, for they got too high up. The Indian, Johnny, stood
on some fallen logs at the foot of the tree, and I sat about
twenty feet above him on the steep hill side, when we heard
a crashing of the underbrush close to us, and the old bear showed
herself ; but, as the cubs did not cry out, she did not come down on
us, and after looking at each other for some time we withdrew.
When we got to the large stream at the head of the lake we found
it greatly swollen and most difficult to cross, and after a cold
swim gained the opposite bank and reached our camp, where I
saw Kinbaskit perched on a rock close to my tent, and taking my
jacket off, gave it a shake to knock off the mud, &c., when my
revolver, which was in the pocket, went off, striking the rock
within a foot of Kinbaskit, who took it very coolly. The next day
we had returned to the camp in the afternoon, when the Indians
saw a black bear on the opposite shore of the lake, and went after
it ; but came back informing me they had wounded the animal,
and wished to go after him next day. So I told them to do so,
thinking a little fresh meat would be an assistance to our limited
supplies.   Kinbaskit and the two Indians soon returned with the
bear, but poor Kinbaskit was rather badly wounded, which
occurred, as the Indians told me, in the following way. They
traced the wounded animal by the blood, and found him lying
alongside a log. Kinbaskit thought he was so badly wounded
he could do no harm, and advanced with only a heavy stick
in his hand to despatch him ; but when quite close the bear
suddenly stood up on his hind legs and struck Kinbaskit with one
of his paws, giving him severe wounds on the scalp and tearing
the flesh of his arm and hand very badly, when the Indian, Tim,

ing a
t find.
of a
aining
moun-
r ; we
ng up
with a
, stood
about
heard
aowed
wn on
ndrew.
found
a cold
here I
ig my
en my
rock
xt day
ndians
after
animal,
lo so,
mited
h the
which
They
lying
anded
stick
bear
h one
earing
Tim,

shot the bear dead. It was quite a surgical work, sewing and plastering up the old chief's wounds, who appeared quite unconcerned. A temporary depôt was now made at the north end of the lake. I could not use the boats below this point with safety, the river being full of rapids nearly the whole distance to the "Boat Encampment"; and as I was most anxious to hear how the T party, whom I had sent up the North Thompson to survey through Yellowhead Pass, were getting on, I sent a member of party S with Indians. I was much disappointed by the almost immediate return of the member of my staff, asserting that he was too unwell to make the journey ; but the Indians went on and returned on the 14th August, informing me they could find no traces of my party as far as the easterly end of Moose Lake, in Yellowhead Pass, at which point they turned back. I then decided to go over myself, and, if necessary, proceed as far as the Tête Jaune Cache.

CHAPTER XXX.

A large quantity of the supplies were at the north end of the lake, and under the able superintendence of my Chief Commissariat Officer and Assistant-Paymaster on the Pacific Coast, Mr. A. S. Hall, whom I put in general charge, as I had perfect confidence in his energy and push, they made good progress during my absence. Mr. A. S. Hall accompanied me in 1871 from Ottawa, when I commenced my surveys, and remained in charge of the commissariat department throughout, returning to Ottawa when the accounts, &c , were being audited On the 27th of August I began the journey, taking three Indians, Charley, a Columbia-river Shuswap, and my two young Indians, Tim and Johnny. We went in as direct a course as possible, Charley being our guide, and commenced at once to ascend a steep mountain side to get a shorter way to Mount Brown, and avoid the thick undergrowth. &c., which we should encounter in the Columbia valley We had a most fatiguing climb up the steep, thickly-wooded mountain side , the black flies were tormenting, the day was excessively hot, and though there was perpetual snow far above us and the Columbia in sight below, not a drop of water could we obtain. We suffered very much, particularly two of the Indians who had light packs. At last they laid down, and Charley and I went on a short distance, and sat down to rest. I scooped a cool stone out of the ground, and put it against my throat to see if it would improve matters, when Charley jumped up, exclaiming, "Chuck"—which is "water." We hurried on, and presently came to a fine cascade of ice-cold water, into which our heads went, and we quenched our almost intolerable thirst. I sent Charley back with a can of water to the other Indians, who soon made their appearance, and having enjoyed the water, we all laid down on the moss, and slept soundly till daylight, when we resumed our journey, and crossing a high ridge, from which the view was magnificent, particularly of the Selkirk Mountains, where we could see hundreds of snow-capped peaks. We now commenced a steep descent by the valley of a mountain torrent, thickly covered with a fine growth of large timber, having, on reaching the bottom of the valley, to wade through an abominable swampy forest with underbrush, where the thick water, of a colour like rusty iron, made it imperative on reaching the Wood, or Portage River, to jump in to clean ourselves. We then followed the southerly side of the stream for some distance through heavy timber, and, tying a few logs together, crossed the river and camped. Going on in the morning for some distance through a thick forest we reached the gravel beds of the river, which are covered at high water. We waded the river many times, and camped at the foot of Mount Brown, opposite the old camping ground of the H. B. Company, where Mr. Charles, one of the company's officers, was accidentally shot many years ago. Here we made a good supper, thanks to a porcupine we had killed. We now began the steep ascent by the old H. B. Company's trail to reach the depression between Mounts Brown and Hooker—the "Athabasca Pass"—gaining an elevated valley, with grassy glades and groves of firs. Where the walking was fair we made good headway, and camped a short distance north of the celebrated "Committee's Punch-Bowl." Charley killed a cariboo, and we took the fresh skin with the hair on it to make moccassins, as we were sorely in need of something to put on our feet, and cached the meat by making a platform high up three trees, and peeled the bark off to prevent those cunning little thieves, the wolverins, from getting it. Following along, and gradually ascending Mount Brown, we saw a grizzly bear above us, and shot a ptarmigan, and then coming on a well-beaten cariboo trail, reached the top of a ridge with a high conical peak immediately on our right, and a mass of hard perpetual snow on the north side of the ridge, down which we went with difficulty, seeing the fresh tracks of four cariboo. There was a fine view from the top of this ridge, the mountains to the north forming a

G

magnificent amphitheatre, some five miles in width, and the innumerable torrents dashing down the rocks, with the white foam like silver spray, the thick groves of dark firs, the grassy glades and many small lakes, or ponds, rendering it enchanting. On reaching the bottom of the snow, I told Charley he had better try and kill a cariboo, and we would camp a quarter mile further on. He did not seem disposed to go, and I said I thought he was afraid he could not get one. This put that celebrated mountain hunter's blood in a glow, when he said in Chinook, "Nika clatawa—quansum mameluce—potlach mika musket;" or, "I go—always kill—give me your rifle." I handed him the gun, and he was off like a shot. We went on a short distance and camped, hearing two shots in rapid succession, and shortly after Charley walked into camp with the hind leg of a cariboo, and, in answer to a question from one of the Indians, he said, "Mameluce mox" ("I have killed two"); and produced two tongues, which were cooked for supper, and found very good.

the
hite
ssy
ting.
had
arter
said
that
said
mika
." I
on a
ssion,
of a
us, he
duced
good.

CHAPTER XXXI.

I wished to examine a little of the valley that crossed, at right angles, the direction in which we were travelling. From what I saw of it, my impression is that there is a pass through from the Canoe to the Whirlpool River, which at some future day may be utilised, but I cannot be quite certain of the pass, as my examination was very limited, and, therefore, imperfect. On my way this morning I was astonished to see two graceful young cariboo come running up a glade with high cliffs on either side, and look at me I did not wish to shoot them, they appeared so tame, so waving my hat they ran off, but kept returning. I shouted, and they ran up to the top of the rocks, trotting about ; at last they ran down some distance off, and passed behind a large rock, trotting. I could not resist the temptation of a flying shot, when they sprang out of sight, and I supposed I had missed, but one of my Indians, who had followed me, said "Tenass mowick mamcluce "—" The little deer is killed," and, sure enough, on going to the spot I found the poor thing dying with my bullet through its neck. I could not but feel thoroughly ashamed of myself for wantonly killing such a beautiful creature. Crossing the range ahead of us, through a wide grassy depression, we came to some small ponds surrounded with bold mountains and most picturesque scenery. Out of the ponds flows a stream away to the north, which we followed through a park-like valley for some distance, and then, as it rapidly increased in size, we found it dash and roar through wild chasms and a rough country, until it forms a junction, a short distance west of Yellowhead Lake, with the stream flowing out of it. The stream I followed is the true source of the Fraser River, and I had thus been within a comparatively short space of time at the source of the two large rivers of the Pacific

Coast, the Columbia and the Fraser. The country became very rough, but for a long distance we got on a narrow open ledge that much helped us, as it was clear of timber, and like a pathway four or five feet in width. My feet were dreadfully sore, and we had still to pass through some timber, where the fire had been quite recently, and the burnt moss was still hot and many fires smouldering. At last we reached the foot of the valley and waded the stream. Our delight can be imagined when we came on a newly-cut trail, and prepared to have a meal, but just then the tinkling sound of a mule bell greeted our ears, and a minute after I was in the midst of a train of animals that I found belonged to my trail party in charge of Mr. William C. McCord, then camped on Yellowhead Lake. I asked the head packer his name, and he told me MacBrown; this struck me as a peculiar name. I asked him how he came by it, and he told me that in the previous year, wishing to join the parties under Mr. Roderic McLennan on his expedition to Moose Lake, he found nearly all the parties were Macs, so he thought he should have a better chance of employment if he were a Mac too, and therefore substituted MacBrown for Brown. I secured a horse from him. and a few minutes afterwards passed through the trail party's camp, and went on to where the men were at work; both McCord and the men were surprised to see me make my appearance by the valley I had followed. Ascertaining that my survey party was in the neighbourhood of Moose Lake, I sent for the engineer in charge, and pulling my boots off my nearly crippled feet, had a good rest or the remainder of the day.

very
dge
e a
ully
the
and
lley
ame
just
d a
at I
m C.
head
e as
l me
Mr.
ound
ve a
efore
him.
amp,
d the
ley I
the
arge,
l rest

VIEW OF THE CANADIAN ROCKY MOUNTAINS, WITH BOW RIVER, ON THE ROUTE OF THE CANADIAN PACIFIC RAILWAY.

CHAPTER XXXII.

That evening, Mr. Mohun, the Engineer-in-charge of party T, Mr. McCord and myself had a long talk over all the proceedings that had gone on since I left them, and learning that Mr. Sandford Fleming, the Engineer-in-chief of the Canadian Pacific Railway, had not as yet passed through, I took four horses and began to make my way, with the Indians, through the valley of the "Miette," which at that time without a trail was most unpleasant for the greater portion of the distance. In going along the bank in a place where the trees were very thick, a horse with all our provisions tumbled into the stream, and we could not induce him to come out; he seemed to enjoy the cool water and freedom from flies it afforded him. At last we went on to a small rapid close by and camped, ringing the bell to attract him, and he waded down and came out, and we then got our supper. That rapid I named " Horse Rapid," of which more anon. Another hard forenoon's work brought us to the Athabasca, which we struck at the beautiful site of the old Hudson Bay Fort, Henry House, which had entirely disappeared with the exception of a hole that represented the former cellar, and a pile of stones that had once been a chimney. This old fort was at the junction of the two routes followed by the early trappers and by the Hudson Bay Company ; one route going by the Tête Jaune, or Yellowhead Pass, the other by the Whirlpool River, Committee's Punch-Bowl, &c., to the Boat Encampment, and known as the "Athabasca Pass." We journeyed on, admiring the scenery, and came to Snaring River. Here for a short time we were at a loss to find a ford, but succeeded in getting over, though, as we found afterwards, by the wrong ford, and followed a trail by the river that was bad in places. At last, on reaching an open bench, we came upon the main trail and saw the track of boots, which the Indians at once said were "Moncasses," or men from the east, unaccustomed to mountain travelling. I sent an Indian back on my horse with a note, as I felt almost certain it was Mr Fleming's party, and walked back to Snaring River and camped. The Indian returned after dark and brought me a note from Mr. Fleming, that set all doubts at rest; we had missed each other, as I took the river and the other party the other trail.

From a very old but active woman named Marguerite, whom I afterwards saw at Jasper House, I heard the following story. Many years ago, before the introduction of firearms in the mountains, there was a small tribe of Indians, who captured the mountain sheep, the wood buffalo, and the bear by snaring them, and had their principal residence on this river, which gave it the name of "Snaring River." A party of Assineboines, who had obtained firearms from the traders in the east, invaded this little band, and shooting all the Indians, they carried off he women and children, and having skinned the dead Indians took their skins to trade with the whites, but the old lady was unable to inform me if they made a profitable trade with the skins

At daylight I followed and overtook the party just as they were entering the valley of the "Miette," and I had the pleasure of forming the acquaintance of the Rev Principal Grant and Dr. Marvin, Mr. Fleming and his son Frank were old acquaintances. We dined on the bank of the river, and camped at "Horse Rapid.' In the evening Mr. Fleming treated us to a glass of punch and a cigar, and the toasts, "The Queen" and "The Dominion" were duly drank In the morning, being Sunday, we went on a short distance to McCord's camp, where the Rev Dr. Grant held divine service, and we passed a pleasant afternoon. We went on the next day, expecting to reach the camp of party T in good time. Dr Marvin and I went ahead to have supper ready, but a drizzling rain came on, and a very dark night. Hour after hour passed before we reached the camp. Once there, we got supper ready, and waited for the others. At last we concluded that they must have camped, and we lay down, but after a time they began to straggle in, wet cold, and hungry, and consequently not in the best of humours. In the morning, after a good breakfast, we parted, they to continue their journey to the Pacific, I to go back to the Columbia River. On my way back to McCord's camp, which had moved some miles easterly since I left it, a severe thunderstorm, with vivid lightning, came on, and we got a thorough drenching, the rain before I reached the camp turning into snow. The next day I reached the ford across the Athabasca River, and camped. Here I left everything I could possibly do without in a cache; putting my ammunition and such things as I wanted into a canvas bag, and what I did not require in a similar one ; then having forded the river, I got on an old trail, which proved to be the wrong one, and had to camp in the woods. In the morning we found traces of the old trail, and made good progress. We met a cinnamon bear, who came running straight for my horse's head, evidently not seeing us, and when some twenty feet off turned up the mountain One of my Indians, having my rifle at the time, ran after him, and fired a couple of shots, but without effect. A short distance further on I saw some cariboo deer, about thirty or forty, and took one canvas bag off to get out some cartridges, but sad to relate, the wrong bag had been brought from our last cache at Henry House, and we had not a single cartridge. I got off, and led my horse close up to the herd, and it was a pretty sight to see the old and young playing about. They are very graceful animals, and provided they do not smell you, not very timid. We had nothing for it but to see them go off. On we went, finding some fresh fallen snow in the woods, and camping not far from the Committee's Punch-Bowl.

CHAPTER XXXIII.

Expecting to meet party S at the foot of Mount Hooker, I went down the mountain as fast as possible, but could find nothing of them, and urged my weary horses through the stream in many places, being most anxious, as the winter was near at hand. Just as the day was beginning to fade away we thought of making a cut off over the long spur of the mountain that runs down to the south of the Boat Encampment, and led our horses over the rocks and through the woods until we could not see, and then lay down cold, wet, and miserable, with our poor horses without anything to eat. Before daylight, as I lay shivering in a wet blanket, I thought I heard a bell, and awoke one of the Indians, who soon said, "Nawitka, ting-ting."—"Yes, a bell." We led our animals down to the river, and waded along it until I heard the sound of an axe on a high bank of the river, and called out. Then I recognised one of my men, who told me that Mr Green, then in charge of the party, was there, and he came and told me that owing to my long absence, and the near approach of winter, they had concluded that they could not go to the Athabasca that year, and had just began to build a depôt to winter in. I told him to knock off the work and get the men into camp, as we would go on to the Athabasca that autumn. The party were at once set to work to open a short trail through the woods, and we got the animals and a portion of the cargo on the way to the foot of Mount Hooker on the 2nd of October. I now left them to get through as fast as possible, and returned to the Athabasca, which I reached on the 5th October, and found McCord and his party just commencing to build the depôt, afterwards known as the "Athabasca Depôt." From him I learnt that party T had probably left on their return to Victoria, and followed on the next day in hopes of catching them   On reaching the "Grand Forks of the Fraser" I met a mule train, and from the packers ascertained that there was no chance of my overtaking them.   This sudden and unforeseen return of that party sadly interfered with my operations, and was the cause of material delay in the surveys.   I sent a messenger after them, and returning by the depôt went on and brought party S as soon as possible to the summit of the Rocky Mountains in the Yellowhead Pass, and continued the survey easterly from that point on the 24th October.   Our buildings were making good progress, and as the winter had set in it was advisable to kill the cattle we had brought with us from the Columbia River, as they would only get poor after the snow fell, so some of us had a grand hunt, and, owing to their wildness, had to shoot them wherever they could be found.

The weather now began to get very cold indeed, and I took a trip down to Jasper House to examine the country.   I then first saw that remarkable point of the mountains opposite this old trading post of the B. Company   The glory of Jasper House had departed, for in place of the picturesque buildings described by Dr Hector, and since pulled down, I found replaced by two wretched little log cabins.   The point of the mountains opposite the house, referred to above, is known as "Roche à Miette," or "Miette's Rock," and from old Marguerite I learnt the following story —At the time when the buffalo, the moose, and other large game was plentiful in Jasper valley, an enterprising Frenchman named "Miette" pushed his way into this valley, and followed his trapping avocations with success. One day, seized with a desire to get to the top of the rock, he, after a most difficult and dangerous climb, succeeded.   The venturesome Miette then sat on the edge of the cliff, dangling his legs over it and smoked a pipe, enjoying the fine view his elevated station afforded , and from that day it has been known as "La Roche à Miette " by the Indian and half-breed hunters. I passed the night in Jasper House, where there was only one single room, and I had therefore some dozen Iroquois half-breeds, men, women and children, to keep me company.   They were very quiet, extremely civil, and the men fine, handsome, athletic fellows. They presented me with some Rocky Mountain sheep meat, which was a great treat; and I ordered my Indians to cook them a good meal out of my scanty stores, which they enjoyed very much, appearing rather puzzled to make out what kind of a drink coffee was. Returning to the depôt, the reports of the progress of the pack trains and supplies were favourable; but the men engaged in the transport service found the cold and snow, and consequent want of feed for the animals, was beginning to tell on them. However, there was nothing for it but to keep them there a little longer, so I sent word to bring the supplies to a point some thirty-five miles from our depôt, and then take all the animals into the Jasper valley. I was very anxious about the animals, as their loss would cause a most serious delay in the progress of the work for a long time, if not stop it altogether. We made good progress with the survey, though the weather at times was unpleasantly cold and windy. A few days before the survey reached the "Fiddle River" Christmas Day came on. I had previously sent a few animals to the depôt for some supplies, of which we were very short; but the ice not being sufficiently strong on the Athabasca River, the animals had been detained, and a good dinner for Christmas Day was problematical. I paid a visit on Christmas Eve to the survey camp, to have a talk and smoke with the staff, some of whom were bewailing the loss of a dinner on the following day, so I invited them down to partake of the luxuries in my camp, about two miles away. My stores consisted at that time of some pemmican, flour, and tea, without sugar. I had several courses prepared, the first being pemmican raw, the second pemmican boiled, and in due season the dessert, which was pemmican fried; and my guests looked somewhat disappointed when I informed them they saw all the luxuries before them, and the only thing we could do was to have a good smoke, as I had plenty of tobacco, and try and keep warm. The survey being completed to Fiddle River on the 2nd of January, and it being impossible to proceed any further with it then, I ordered the trail party to build a small depôt there, and having picked out a favourable place at the north-west end of Lac à Brûlé to winter the larger portion of the animals, I returned to the Athabasca depôt, instructing the survey party to follow. I made an examination of a portion of the valleys of the Rock River, opposite Jasper House, and of the Maligne River, nearly opposite the Athabasca depôt, to see if a line for a railway could be obtained through either of them to the North Saskatchewan, but found the valleys impracticable for the purpose. We passed the time pleasantly in our depôt, and prepared the plans, reports, &c., of the survey for transmission to Ottawa. My hunters kept us well supplied with plenty of the wild mountain sheep, upon which we feasted; and the dog-sleighs, kindly sent me by Mr. Chief-Factor Hardisty from Edmonton, brought the supplies left on the Whirlpool River in the previous autumn. The aurora borealis was, on the fine clear nights, a most magnificent spectacle; and many an hour of those long nights I passed watching it. On the arrival of the last of the dog-sleighs from the little depôt on the Whirlpool River, I found that the man left in charge of it—who, though a good workman, was "a bit of a humbug,"—had his feet slightly frozen on the way down. This was, however, owing to his penurious nature, as he would not go to the expense of buying socks and moccasins, or boots, of which we had a plentiful supply. He sent for me, being dreadfully frightened of losing his feet. Seeing, however, there was nothing serious, I made him put his feet in cold water, telling him it was entirely his own fault, and as I had no intention of having any of my men laid up on account of their own foolishness, I should stop his pay and charge him for his board as long as he was an invalid. Nothing more was heard of frozen hands or feet after this, and I noticed the man all right next day chopping firewood in the woods. My head storekeeper, Mr R. M. Rylatt, an ex-sergeant of the Royal Engineers, who came to British Columbia with the corps under the command of Colonel Moody, R.E., in 1858, kept a full table of meteorological observations. The general deductions from them are given in one of Mr. Fleming's reports, when he was Engineer-in-Chief of the Canadian Pacific Railway, and give information regarding the climate, &c., &c.

Discharging the half-breeds, who had worked well and faithfully in charge of the dog-sleighs, I sent them back to Edmonton, and by them the plans, reports, &c., to be forwarded *via* Winnipeg to Ottawa; and I afterwards found that they reached their destination safely. The same day I went to Fiddle River depôt to prepare for the resumption of the survey eastwards

CHAPTER XXXIV.

A report from an explorer, which had been left me by Mr. Fleming's party in the previous autumn, described the country from the easterly end of Lac à Brûlé as "an almost level sandy plain, affording great facilities for railway building." I thought, seeing this, we might run the line quickly to the Saskatchewan, and have ample time to rectify the hurried and most unsatisfactory survey made by party T west of the summit of the Yellowhead Pass ; but my hopes were brought to an end when I started from Fiddle River, for the very first thing I came against was a high ridge, and picking out the lowest depression in it, I directed the line to be carried over it, and made a hasty trip to find the expected level plain. We took two dog-sleighs, but, there being no snow on the flat and side of the hill beyond Fiddle River, Louis, one of the Iroquois hunters, sent back for his two daughters to pack the loads to the top of the ridge. One of the girls, who was a tall and very powerful young woman, took an enormous load without any difficulty, and, on the party crossing the ridge, we came to a large pond some two hundred yards in width and a long way round. There was about six inches of water on the ice, so telling the Indians and half-breeds to camp in the woods on the opposite side, as night was coming on, I sat down, thinking, that as I must get wet feet, I might as well have a smoke and get to camp by time the fire was burning and the supper cooked. I saw the huge woman wading back, and wondered why she was returning, but soon found out, for she told me her father had sent her to pack me over the ice. I had travelled by every known mode, but to be packed by a woman was a novelty, so I protested ; but she insisted, saying I was much lighter than the load she had just packed over, and if she did not take me her father would be very angry ; so I resigned myself to my fate, and was ignominiously packed over. Louis was very proud of the girl's strentgh, and that evening, as we were smoking a pipe, he pointed out the great advantages in having such a powerful girl, and, as he wished to get a horse I had, he made me an offer to make an exchange—I to give him the horse and a few other things, and take the girl instead, to which she did not object, but as I had no idea of becoming a permanent resident of that country, and hardly liked the idea of presenting her in the civilised world, I was obliged to decline what might have turned out a troublesome investment in the end.

On reaching the mouth of Prairie River, I saw that the country was very different to what I expected, and as the snow, except in places, had disappeared, I returned, examining the Athabasca for a short distance and the north side of Lac à Brûlé, along which a good line for a railway may be obtained. At a cañon, a short distance from the mouth of the Prairie River, where the banks are high and a slide had taken place, I noticed very thin seams of bright, brittle lignite, with intervening layers of ironstone mixed with clay. The party had carried the line over the ridge when I returned, but as the grade was heavy, a line was run round the face of it to find an easier grade, but it went by some very unsatisfactory sandhills. Knowing, however, that I could connect it from the opposite side of the Athabasca with a good line, I continued it to save time, and followed the south side of the Athabasca, running it to Hardisty creek, so that a line on either side of the river could make a fresh start eastwards from a common point. I was camped at this creek with one of my young Indians, whom I had brought up with me from New Westminster, when he told me he wished to be paid off, and get a horse, a gun, ammunition, and some provisions, &c., instead of money. This was decidedly very inconvenient, as he had been with me a long time, was a capital cook, packer, hunter, and fisherman. On pressing him for his reasons he told me he wanted to marry the " big woman " for whom I would not trade the horse. I refused his request, and he was very sulky. The next day, Sunday, only Louis and the young Indian being with me, the former complained

of being sick, and I took my rifle and strolled along the river
until the evening. On my return, I found that Louis had left
and gone after his people to the Smoky River, and my Indian, Tim,
in an excessively bad humour. They had evidently made up their
minds as to the marriage, &c., and for having at first refused the
female property myself, and afterwards prevented my servant from
obtaining it, or rather her, my sins were now being visited upon
me. I crossed over to the McLeod River, taking four horses, and
examined a portion of that valley and the ridge between the
Athabasca and McLeod Rivers, and found it very high. On my
return, we followed the Athabasca River for some distance on
the ice, which appeared strong, but suddenly a great area of it
fell two or three feet, the water not yet having risen enough to
support it, and we had some little trouble in getting our horses
up the slope to the bank of the river. The survey progressed
over a rough and unsatisfactory country, crossing the ridge at the
first available point ; always keeping the line for a lower and more
northernly one in view. We had hitherto enjoyed fine weather,
and were camped at the summit of the ridge in a thick growth of
large spruce and black pine, when in the forenoon the sky was
completely overcast, and, becoming very dark, the rain began to
fall. We stopped work and lit a fire under the large forest trees,
waiting for the rain to stop, but it rather increased, and we made
for our camp, getting a thorough drenching. As evening came on,
the rain turned to snow, and the wind rose until it blew a gale.
We lay in our tents, the trees falling on all sides, expecting each
moment to be crushed to death. A tree fell across the tent in
which my transit-man and leveller lay, but fortunately did not
hurt them, as their tent was pitched alongside a very large fallen
tree, which saved their lives. The top of another tree broke off
and struck through a tent of three French Canadians, falling
between them and becoming imbedded about four feet in the
soft ground It was a dreadful night, and the storm did not
abate until the next day. In the morning we cut down the most
dangerous-looking trees, and passed a wretched day. Our animals
had run off, and it was quite a work to find them, some having

gone into the open land along the Athabasca, whilst others had gone to the valley of the McLeod. We next continued the line down into the valley of the McLeod, through thick woods of black pine and spruce. One day, the dinner being over, we were going on with the work, when, as I was ahead with two axemen, we heard a terrific roaring sound, and saw a sheet of flame close to us; we ran back to get on a murkey (a swamp) close to the line, the fire close after us, but before we could reach the party in the rear most of them had bolted back along the line, and were thus travelling in the direction in which the fire was going. After a time I tried to go on with the work, but could not find most of the party, so we made for camp, where we found them all safely. As they had gone in the same direction as the fire, they had a hard run to escape it, and were much tired out.

I now sent a train to Fort Edmonton to procure some supplies of which we were short, as well as beef, cattle, and a few additional men. There were still lingering touches of the old scurvy, and I was suffering from a long attack of dysentery, so I instructed the man in charge to get a few gallons of whisky or other spirits. Our train with the supplies did not arrive for a few days, and the cattle some time afterwards. It was on a Saturday afternoon when the train arrived, bringing two gallons of high wines, of which I took a half-pint bottle, and distributed the rest among the men. At this time I was very weak and could hardly drag my legs over the fallen timber to pick out the line ahead of the party, so I got a cup of water and laid down in my tent sipping the diluted spirit as fast and as strong as I could drink it; at last I felt a pleasant glow come over me and fell asleep, not waking until the morning, when I felt as well as I had ever felt in my life. The men told me the dose I gave them completely drove the scurvy away, and I never heard any more complaints of it. On account of the flies our work was most disagreeable. The survey having reached a point not far from the Pembina River I met " Valad," a half-breed, with instructions from Mr Fleming, and at once discontinued the survey easterly, much to the delight of the party, who were all *en route* for the West next morning.

H

CHAPTER XXXV.

After remaining a day to settle with and discharge the men going to Edmonton, I followed the party. On arriving at the Athabasca depôt the animals were all shod for the mountain work, and leaving a man in charge of the depôt and stores not required for the survey, I proposed to proceed from Moose to Cranberry Lake. We went on to a point a short distance west of Moose Lake, where there was a good crossing for a bridge We now continued the survey and obtained a good line to connect with the line run up the North Thompson and Albreda Rivers. A very curious circumstance occurred just after commencing this survey. I had crossed over to the north side of the river, and went to a small prairie on the trail, when I noticed some men and animals coming from the west, and soon recognised an old acquaintance, who handed me a letter, which he was telling me had been sent up for delivery by Mr. Marcus Smith, then in full charge of railway works, &c, in British Columbia. I had not opened the letter, when a man on horseback came on the prairie emerging from the woods on the east side, whom I at once recognised as Valad, and he handed me a letter from Mr. Fleming, written at Ottawa, and conveying in substance the same instructions as were contained in Mr. Smith's letter. The fact of one being written at Ottawa, and the other at Victoria, and both reaching me at the same time, formed a curious coincidence.

On bringing the survey to an end, the party proceeded on their way to Kamloops, and I made a short exploratory trip up the North Thompson river to see if a pass could be found through the mountains westward to Quensel Lake. I did not succeed in finding a pass there, and returned to the forks of the Thompson and Albreda Rivers, where lay an old canoe. Into this we jumped and ran the Thompson River to a prairie at " Blue River," where

nen
the
tain
not
to
t of
We
rect
. A
this
and
and
old
me
full
not
irie
cog-
ing,
ruc-
one
ioth

heir
orth
the
ling
and
ped
here

we overtook the whole party, and thence went on to Kamloops. Before crossing the river the last instructions ever given me relative to the Canadian Pacific Railway, were issued to Mr A. S. Hall, and I again took up my abode with Mr. John Tait at the Hudson Bay Company's Fort. From Kamloops I went on as fast as possible to Victoria, where I had the pleasure of meeting Mr. Marcus Smith, and after a short stay there Mr. Smith and I went to San Francisco. The weather was extremely boisterous, and Mr. Smith can well say whether it was a pleasant voyage. We duly reached Ottawa about the first week in January, 1874, and I found that my plans, &c., had arrived at the office, as I sent them over by Wells, Fargo & Co.'s express. There being no room for me in the office, I secured a room in the Parliament Buildings, and conveyed all my plans to it that evening. I then went to the Russell House for dinner, which I had just finished when a boy ran in calling out "The Pacific Office is burning up." I ran at once to the old guard-house in the Parliament Building grounds, which was used for the railway offices, and saw them in a mass of flames and pieces of paper and maps flying through the air. A vast amount of valuable information was thus lost to the country, and Mr. Fleming much hampered, as many details for his reports were destroyed.

CHAPTER XXXVI.

I now turned my attention to the Red River and the country tributary to it, and arrived at Winnipeg in the spring of 1875. We landed at the Hudson's Bay Company's Warehouse, at the mouth of the Assiniboine, adjoining Fort Garry   The mud was the most tenacious I ever saw, for all the world like a mixture of tar and grease. Winnipeg at that time was by no means imposing; the buildings, with few exceptions, were of wood, and generally small and badly built   The morning after my arrival, hearing some gentlemen in the hotel talking about the "Big Stony Mountain," I enquired how far it was away, and learning it was only fourteen miles distant, I thought I would take a walk to see it and spend the day climbing about it, as I was tired of looking at the flat monotonous country through which I had travelled.   I walked north through Kildonan, but could see no mountain, and began to fear my eyesight must be failing.   Seeing a man sitting on a fence smoking, I enquired where the "Big Mountain" was, and he pointed out its direction.   I was almost ashamed to admit that I could not see it, when he informed me it was only about five feet high, and I should have to come close before seeing it.   I lit my pipe and chatted with my new acquaintance, who had been many years settled in the country, and was one of Lord Selkirk's original party, and being a Scotchman necessarily very intelligent. He gave me interesting descriptions about the early settlement of the Red River, of the retreat of himself and many of his party into Minnesota for a time, of the massacre of Governor Semple and party close to where we were sitting; of the Red River rebellion, and other information which it was pleasurable to obtain. I then explored a portion of the shores of Lake Winnipeg for coal and minerals.   Coal I found none, but I saw a large deposit on one of the Big Islands of iron ore of the description known as kidney ore, and I saw veins of quartz on the east shore that were mineral-bearing quartz. The rock on the west shore was limestone and very soft sandstone. I saw some very fine fossils in the limestone, and at Gull Point, on Big Island, I also found a meteoric stone about two feet in length and ten or twelve inches in thickness. I visited the Icelandic settlement at Gimli, and was sorry to see the wretched land given to these unfortunate people. In 1876 I undertook a contract to build the first sewers in the City of Winnipeg, which are circular and constructed of wood, and in the spring took a contract to build a tramway for the Hudson Bay Company, over the portage at Grand Rapid, on the Saskatchewan River. Lord and Lady Dufferin paid a visit to this spot, and I took the opportunity of having the last spike driven by Lady Dufferin : it was also the *first spike*, though on a very small railway, *driven in the Canadian North-West*. A tram-car was properly decorated with trees, ornamented deerskins, &c., to convey the Vice-regal party over the road, with an avenue of green fir trees planted at the end of the track. We also managed to make a spike and hammer out of steel, which, with due preparation, looked like silver. Lady Dufferin having driven the spike kept the hammer, which I had thought of appropriating as a memento of the occasion; but it is in better hands.

The white fish and sturgeon at times in the Rapid were very plentiful, and the pike, generally called jack-fish, seemed innumerable. The natives used to scoop up the white fish and pike with scoop nets fastened to a long pole, and the sturgeon they caught by first felling with the end of a pole where they lay, and then reversing the pole, on the other end of which was a strong, sharp iron hook, they would suddenly jerk the sturgeon out, always beginning with the fish lowest down the river, and then with those nearest the shore. In this way I saw five large fellows landed out of a single pool. The fishermen told me that if they were to fell the sturgeon with the iron they would swim off, but they did not appear afraid of the wooden handle, provided it was handled gently. The pike would bite at anything ; I first tried a red rag, but it was so troublesome to replace it after each throw, that I simply threw in the arge hook without anything on it, and they bit just as well.

In 1877 I found the line of the Canadian Pacific Railway was likely to go north, crossing the Red River at Selkirk, the Manitoba Lake at " The Narrows," and thence reach the Pacific by some northerly pass. I therefore commenced an examination of the country, spent the following summer of 1878 in a similar manner, and went to Ottawa to obtain the charters for the lines I proposed These were the present air line of the Canadian Pacific, a branch to connect with the proposed line of the C.P.R. near Selkirk, and the line now known as the South-Western, and the intention to ultimately secure an extension of the line by the route now adopted for the Canadian Pacific through the mountains, and terminating at Burrard Inlet This resulted in the granting of the charter to the South-Western in 1879, and I returned to Manitoba as Chief Engineer of the Company. A short time convinced me that I was associated with an element not congenial, and with a board of directors the reputation of the majority of whom in the commercial world was very bad, and who, I felt certain, would never carry out the work I proposed I therefore decided, at whatever cost, to cut myself entirely clear of them, which I did, and it is gratifying to me now to know that I was not mistaken in so doing, though I have been defrauded out of the whole of my pay, and a large amount that I advanced to make up the first deposit required to properly organise the company.

The Syndicate having undertaken the construction of the Canadian Pacific Railway, I informed some of the leading men in it as to the proper line to adopt through the mountain ranges of British Columbia, and their Engineer, Major A. B Rogers, met me twice, when I gave him the information that has led to the final adoption of the line for the railway by the route I so long and anxiously struggled for, and upon which the success of the railway as a commmercial undertaking is dependent, and the prosperity of British Columbia assured.

The Province of Manitoba being very flat, and any material for building substantial and permanent roads most expensive, I saw that an immense benefit would be conferred upon the country by the construction of electric tramways, which would also be feeders to the Canadian Pacific Railway. So, forming a company, I obtained a charter from the local legislature, but owing to opposition, which it is impossible to understand, I was unable to take the necessary steps to get the system into operation, but have no doubt at some future time the advantages of the proposed system will become so apparent that it will be undertaken by others.

THE END.

Note 1.—In concluding this small book, which has to a great extent been devoted to routes for roads and railways, and the geographical features of portions of the country, I have not touched much on the resources of British Columbia. Others have already done so, and the official report of the Dominion Government of 1883 gives very accurate statistics and information.

As an agricultural country the extent suitable for settlement is limited, but in the valleys, where farming can be carried on, vegetables, grain, and many varieties of fruit are grown and cannot be excelled in quality. In the Selkirk range, and the more southerly portion of the Gold range, the wild fruits of various species grow luxuriantly, and it is to be inferred that when the dense timber and moss with which these mountains are now clothed is cleared off, grapes of a very good quality can be grown, and in the course of time wine will doubtless be one of the products of the country. The fisheries on the coast and in the rivers are unlimited, and almost all the sea-fish found in northern waters abound, excepting the cod, the lobster, and the mackerel. There is, it is true, a species of cod, but different to that caught in the Atlantic; it is known as rock cod. There are other varieties of fish not found in the Atlantic, and I may mention the rich and delicate little oo-la-han as one of them. The timber is magnificent, and is found in large quantities. Iron and coal are of a very superior quality, and enormous deposits exist on Vancouver and the adjacent islands, as well as in other parts of the country. Copper is also found, as well as lead and silver.

The facilities for shipbuilding and making machinery of various kinds, for manufacturing railway iron, &c., are unequalled in the world, while in no portion of the Dominion can a climate be found to compare with that of the most favoured portions of British Columbia.

NOTE 2.—On the eve of sending off my manuscript for publication, I have had the pleasure of reading Mr. Sandford Fleming's last interesting work, "Old to New Westminster," and of seeing the substantial approval such an eminent engineer gives to the line for the Canadian Pacific Railway by that which I from the first recommended to the Crown Colony of British Columbia, and subsequently to that of the Dominion. I cannot, however, but pay a high tribute to the dauntless energy and untiring zeal that has characterised and, I am glad to say, crowned with success the unwearying struggles of my successor in the mountain surveys, Major A. B. Rogers.—W. MOBERLY.

H. BLACKLOCK & Co., Printers, &c., 75, Farringdon Road, London, E.C. (2394.

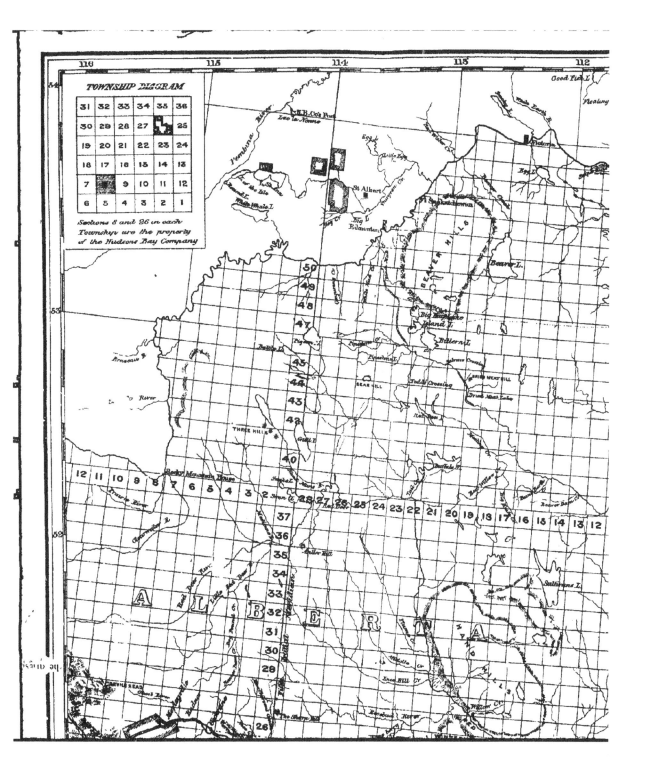

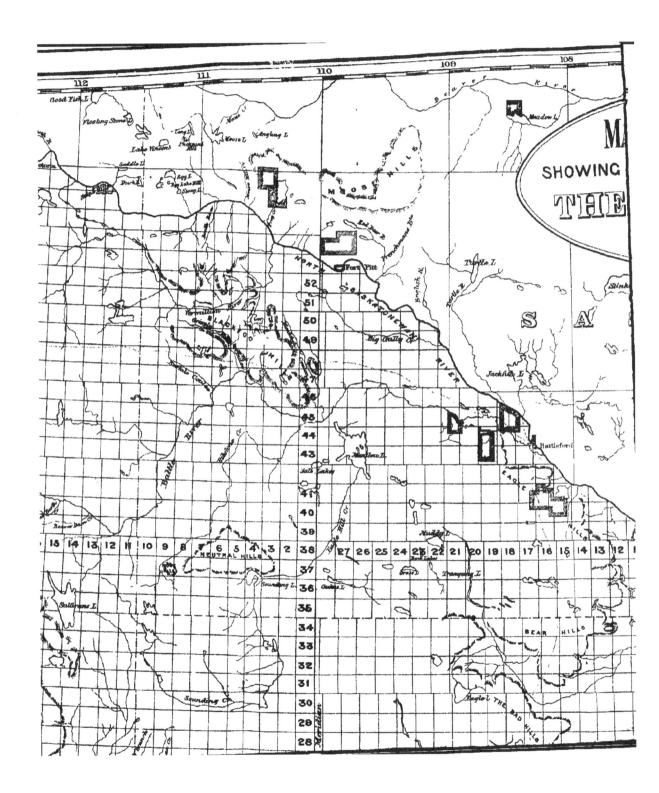

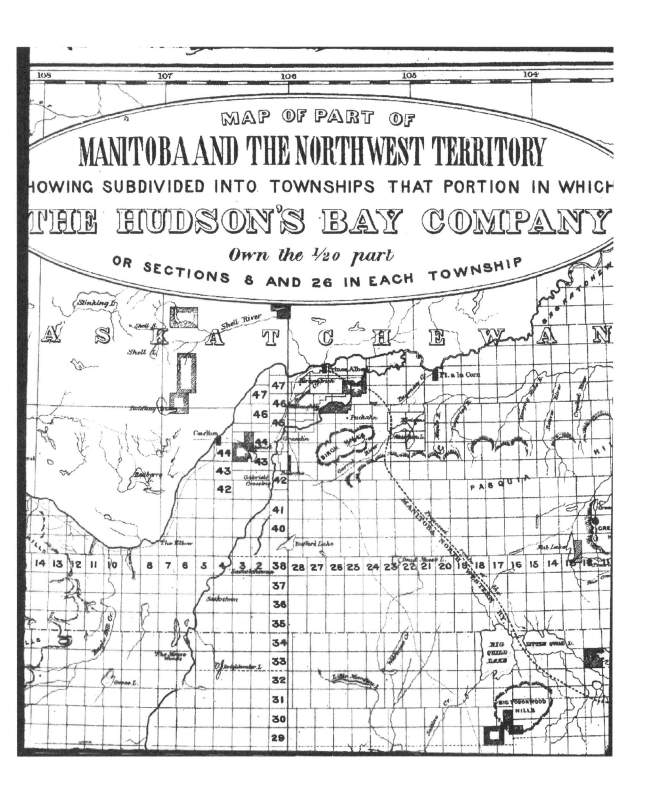

MAP OF PART OF

MANITOBA AND THE NORTHWEST TERRITORY

HOWING SUBDIVIDED INTO TOWNSHIPS THAT PORTION IN WHICH

THE HUDSON'S BAY COMPANY

Own the ¹⁄₂₀ part

OR SECTIONS 8 AND 26 IN EACH TOWNSHIP

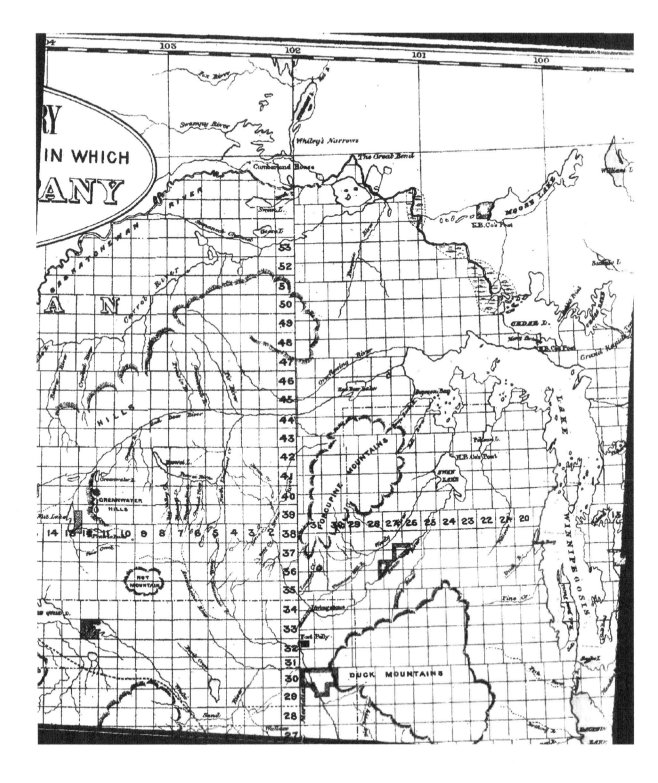

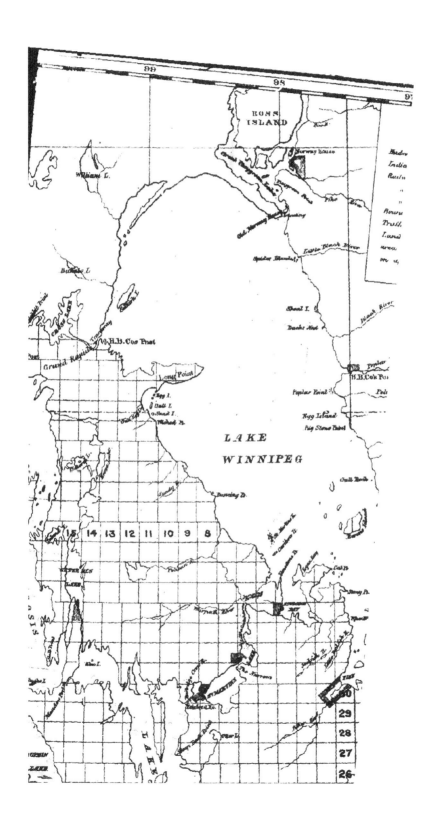

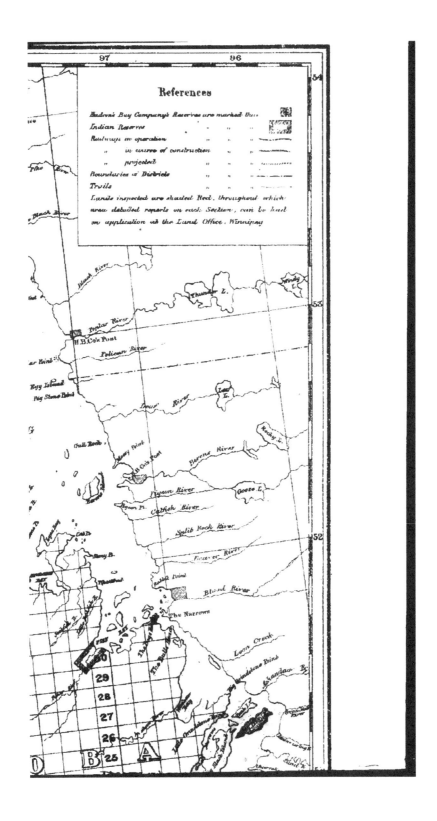

References

Hudson's Bay Company's Reserves are marked thus

Indian Reserves   "   "   "

Railways in operation   "   "   "

    "   in course of construction   "   "   "

    "   projected   "   "   "

Boundaries of Districts   "   "   "

Trails   "   "   "

Lands inspected are shaded Red, throughout which
area detailed reports on each Section, can be had
on application at the Land Office, Winnipeg

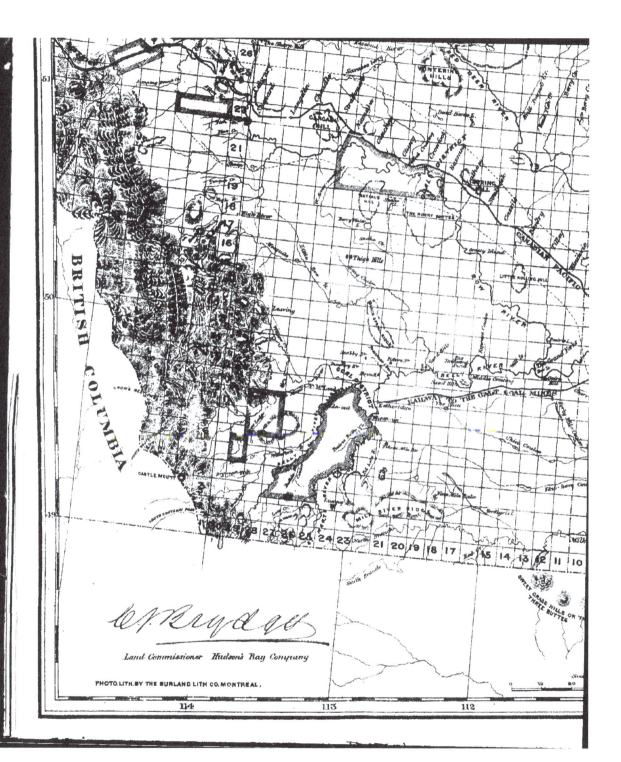

BRITISH COLUMBIA

Land Commissioner   Hudson's Bay Company

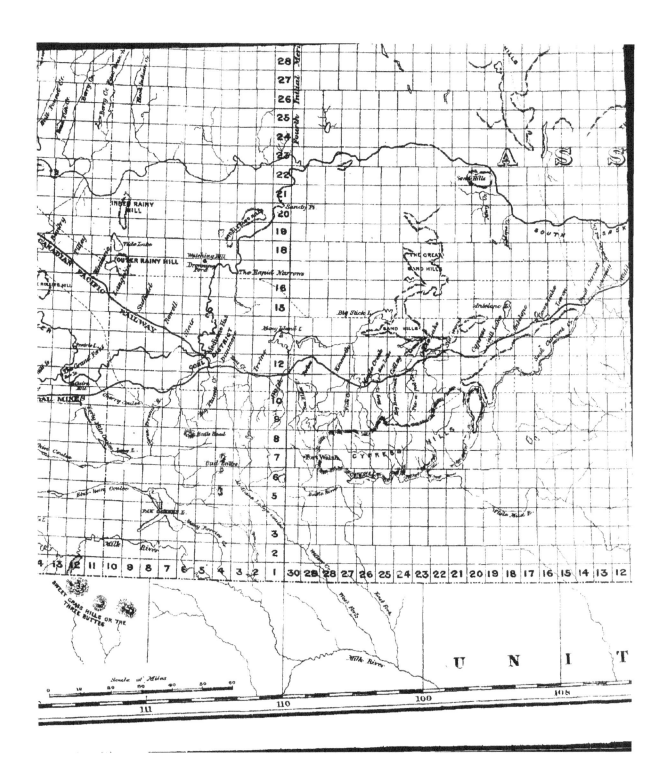

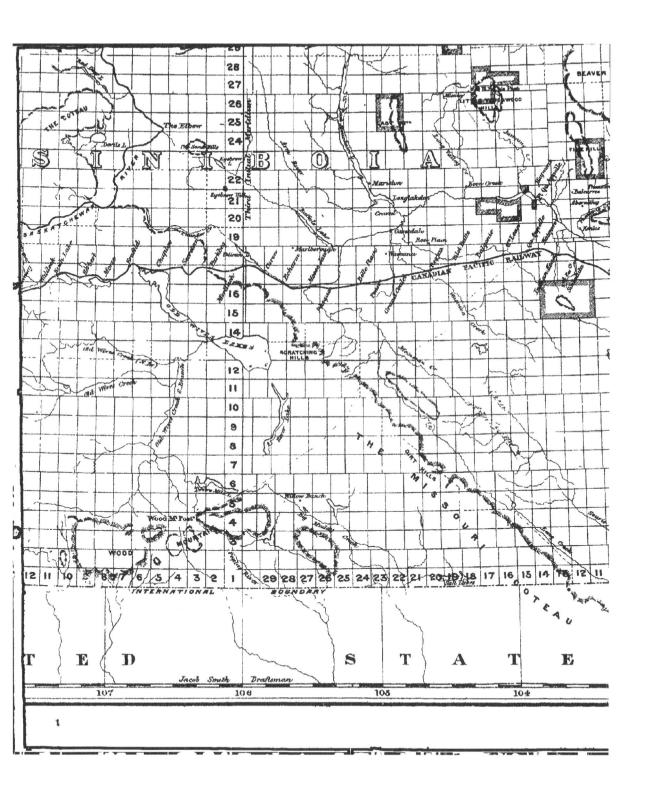

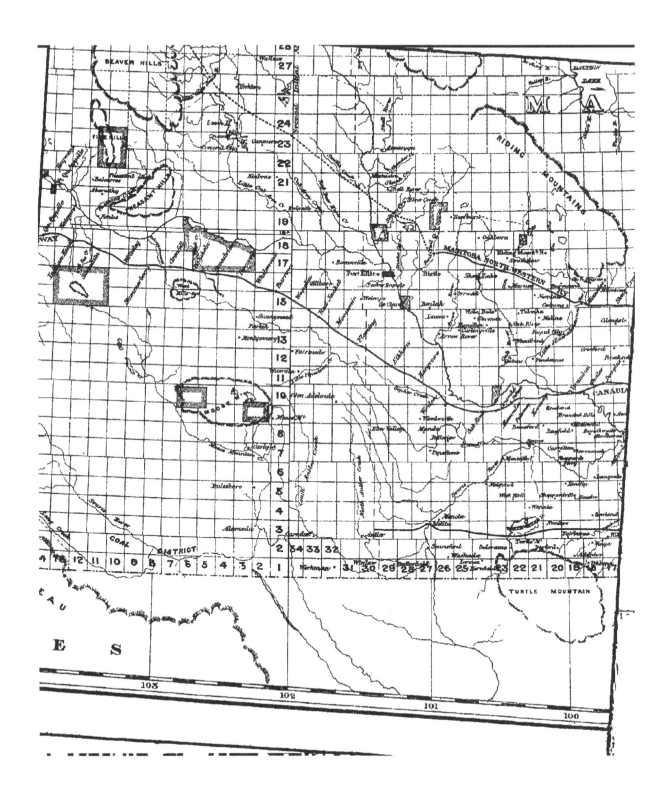

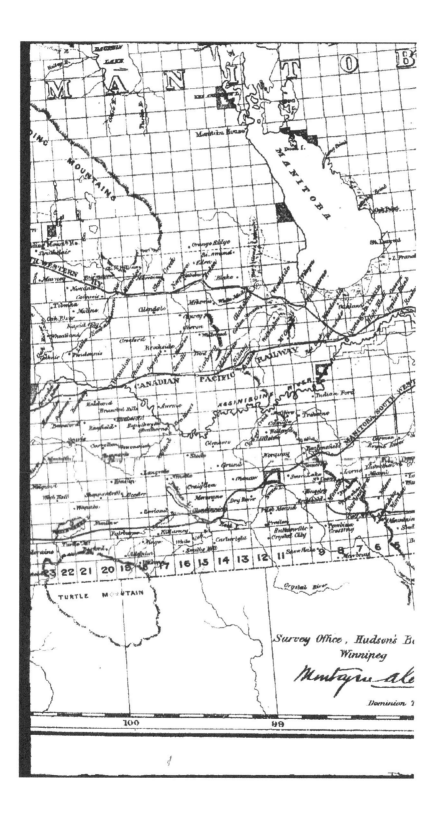

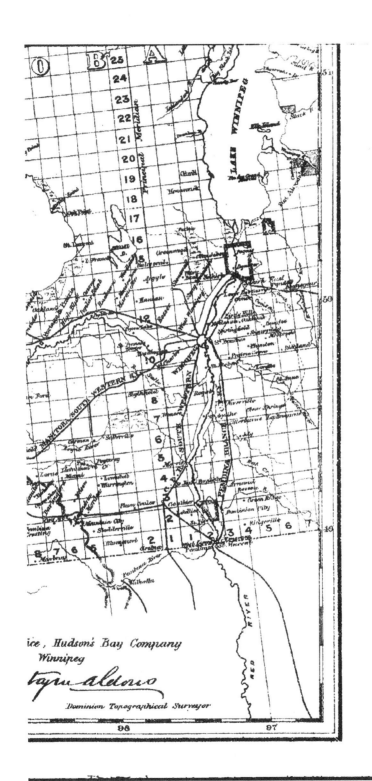

ice, Hudson's Bay Company
Winnipeg

Wm. Aldous

Dominion Topographical Surveyor

the potato a profitable crop even during the first season, immediately after breaking, by turning the sod over on the seed.

The average yield per acre as stated by a number of farmers has ranged from 300 to 320 bushels, and a number have claimed a yield of 400 bushels of potatoes per acre. The average weight per bushel has been from 55 to 60 lbs.

The following statements have been made by farmers based on their actual experiences in Manitoba, and the North West.

W. H. J. Swain, of Morris,
> Has produced 800 to 1000 bushels of turnips to the acre, and 60 bushels of beans have also been raised by him per acre.

S. C. Higginson, of Oakland.
> Has produced cabbages weighing 17½ lbs. each.

Allan Bell, of Portage-La-Prairie,
> Has had cabbages 45 inches around, and turnips weighing 25 pounds each.

Beets.

A good deal of attention is already being paid in different parts of Canada to the cultivation of the sugar-beet and its manufacture into sugar, but there is no part of the Dominion where it can be raised in such paying quantities as in the North-West. The rich soil, the ease with which they can be cultivated, all tend to make the production of beet crops profitable, more especially when, as in the case of the sugar beet, large quantities can be used for manufacturing purposes.

Fruit Culture.

As yet the culture of fruit and apples in the North-West is in its infancy, but there is no doubt that certain varities can be grown successfully. An abundance, however, of wild fruit exists, such as strawberries, raspberries, whortleberries, cranberries, plums, black and red currants, blueberries and grapes, so that there is no scarcity in this respect for the settler, and he will find the flavour of the wild fruit of the North-West most delicious. In Minnesota, not many years ago, it was contended that apple trees would not grow there, and yet to-day the Minnesota apple is a notable product of that State.

Labor.

There is a considerable demand for farm laborers during the greater part of the growing season, when good wages are paid, the average being about $20 per month with board.

In this way settlers, whose means are limited, are often enabled to tide over the first season or two, by working as farm laborers for their neighbors, until such time as the increased product of their own farms requires all their attention.

"The most successful thing is Success."

The following statements made by actual settlers and issued under the authority of the Government, are the best and most convincing proofs of the great advantages offered by Manitoba and Canadian North West, as a most desireable field for immigration.

"I am a native of Western Ontario and have been farming fifteen years. This is my fifth year here, and I much prefer this country to anywhere else. "JAMES STEWART, Meadow Lea."

"I would just say that there are no obnoxious weeds here. When a field is ready to be reaped, as a rule you cannot see anything only grain Flax grows well in this country. I think it can be grown with profit. I have seen it grow as tall as I saw it in Ireland."

"Vegetables of all kinds grow splendidly without much labor and with no manure. "MATHEW OWENS, J. P., High Bluff."

"I have been in the country six years and have found the driest

ely

has
eld
hel

eir

60

25

of
to
in
se
of
ar

n-
s-
v-
d
e-
ne
it
y

r
e

n
r
s

r
g
n

n
o

n
n

d

t

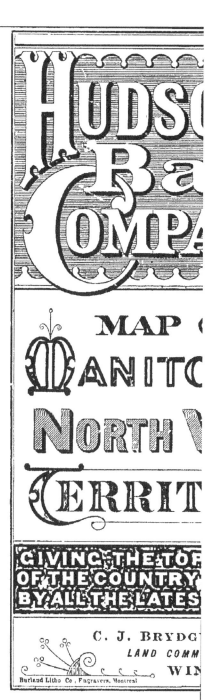

MANITOBA

—AND THE—

NORTH-WEST

The Extent of the Territory.

The Province of Manitoba, in Canada, extends from eastward of the Red River to a line about 200 miles west of that river, and beyond that is the North-West Territory, reaching to the base of the Rocky Mountains, a further distance of nearly 800 miles, which will be divided into four new Provinces

The Red River runs through Manitoba, for upwards of 100 miles to its outlet into Lake Winnipeg

The valley of the Red River contains some of the richest alluvial soil on the continent of North America, and the Assiniboine River, several hundred miles in length, which falls into the Red River at Winnipeg, runs through another valley, having a great depth of rich soil

The Little Saskatchewan River falls into the Assiniboine about 150 miles from its mouth, and runs parallel to the Assiniboine about 60 miles to the east of it

These three rivers in Canadian territory, with their tributaries, comprise an area of wheat and grazing lands estimated at 300 miles long by 150 broad, which produces wheat of the finest quality It is now being settled upon by farmers from Canada and the United States, and by emigrants from Great Britain and Ireland

Municipal Organization and Drainage.

Manitoba has been divided into Municipal Districts, which are now being regularly organized Roads and bridges are being built wherever required, and a regular system of municipal affairs is being put into operation The local government of Manitoba are also putting into force a system of arterial drainage, which will greatly improve those lands which are now wet

School System

In addition to the excellent education now obtainable in the City of Winnipeg, the Government have reserved two sections in each township for school lands, the proceeds of which, as sold, are applied to the establishment of good schools In every part of the country, therefore, as fast as settlement progresses, schools will be provided where good education can be obtained for children

Water Supply

The country is watered by numerous rivers streams, and creeks. Large numbers of lakes and ponds, abounding with wild fowl, exist all over the North West The supply of water is ample, wells only requiring to be sunk to a moderate depth.

Timber and Fuel Supply

The line from Winnipeg to Thunder Bay passes through extensive timber districts near Rat Portage, Eagle River, and other places, where large saw mills are now in operation, which supply at moderate prices lumber required for buildings and fences in the western part of the country.

Considerable quantities of timber for building purposes and for fuel also exist on the banks of most of the rivers and creeks, and there are in addition groves of poplar all over the country

Coal.

Deposits of coal exist on the Saskatchewan Rivers The Company's coal lands have bee inspectors showing large deposits, and their at the office of the Company There will a reached the coal fields, be an ample supply railway will afford ready means of distributin the settled parts of the country. The line Bay will also bring in large supplies of bot tending to keep prices at moderate figures.

Hints as to Capital Re

A settler who wants to take up land in Ma of $2,000 or £400 sterling, secure 160 acres an acre, and provide himself with a reasor barn, stable, pair of oxen, cows and pigs, p that is necessary to give him a fair start and for the future

The taxes are much less than in either the c or Great Britain

In other words, a man with a family can able on a farm for a sum representing less ti of rent and taxes payable in Great Britain an size The payment can be spread over at annual amount due being paid out of the surp would be felt only as an item in his ordinary when these payments are completed, the far perty, without any leasehold or other obligat

By buying land on the reasonable terms o payment, a settler with $500 or $1,000, say establish himself comfortably, and soon bec owner of his land

The Productiveness of

The productiveness of the soil along the R Little Saskatchewan Valleys, is greater than and the yield of wheat per acre is larger Th out the whole Province of Manitoba The cereals and vegetables from Manitoba at agr Toronto, Hamilton, London and Kingston of the fertility and productiveness of the pra The quality of wheat grown is also much sup other part of the continent The grade kno hard" commands in the markets of the world 15 per cent than any other known grade of said of the other cereals and vegetables grow

This excess in the intrinsic value of the pro toba and the North West, in addition to the acre is very nearly double the average of th area of the United States, are most importai by intending settlers.

Quality of Whea

In regard to the quality of the wheat, Pioneer Press, of St Paul, speaks for itself.

"It seems to be a settled fact that the furt up to a certain limit, the better it is

*   *   *   *   *

"The future great wheat region of the world the rich and far-famed valley of the Saskat grows to perfection, not only in quality, but

"The berry obtains an amber color, round

Coal.

n the Saskatchewan, Bow, Belly, and Souris
coal lands have been examined by competent
deposits, and their reports can now be seen
ny. There will a now that the railway has
an ample supply of fuel, and the lines of
means of distributing both coal and timber to
country. The line of railway from Thunder
ge supplies of both timber and coal, thus
moderate figures.

to Capital Required.

take up land in Manitoba can, by an outlay
g, secure 160 acres of land at from $5 or 20s.
self with a reasonably comfortable house,
, cows and pigs, ploughs, harrows, and all
him a fair start and a competency and home

than in either the older Provinces of Canada

with a family can establish himself comfort-
representing less than the average per acre
in Great Britain *annually* for a farm of equal
e spread over at least seven years, and be
paid out of the surplus earnings of the farm,
tem in his ordinary annual expenditure ; and
completed, the farm becomes his own pro-
ld or other obligations.

reasonable terms offered as regards terms of
500 or $1,000, say from £100 to £200. can
ibly, and soon become independent and the

uctiveness of the Soil.

he soil along the Red River, Assiniboine and
eys, is greater than in Minnesota or Dakota.
acre is larger. This is also the fact through-
f Manitoba. The exhibit of the growth of
m Manitoba at agricultural shows at Ottawa,
on and Kingston is the strongest testimony
tiveness of the prairie soil of that Province.
vn is also much superior to that raised in any
t. The grade known as " Man.toba No. 1
narkets of the world a higher price by at least
er known grade of wheat. The same may be
ad vegetables grown in the country.
sic value of the products of the soil of Mani-
in addition to the fact that the product per
the average of the entire wheat producing
are most important facts to be considered

uality of Wheat.

ty of the wheat, the following, from the
l, speaks for itself :

ed fact that the further north wheat is grown,
etter it is.

*　　*　　*　　*　　*

region of the world will undoubtedly be in
ley of the Saskatchewan, where this grain
nly in quality, but in every other particular.
amber color, rounds out into a fullness it does

not attain here, and is rich in gluten, the life sustaining principle of
flour.

*　　*　　*　　*　　*　　*　　*

Some two or three years ago, samples were procured from several
parts of the Province of Manitoba for trial. The best of this was
placed in the hands of some of our leading wheat-growers for cultivation. One variety of Scotch Fife yielded the first year at the rate of
37 bushels to the acre, of a hard amber color, which the wheat in-
spector for the Millers' Association at Minneapolis, pronounced the
finest specimen he had seen since he had been connected with the
association.

" Straw stood up stiff and strong, some of it being over five feet
high, the heads were long, while the color of the growing grain was
superb."

Comparative Yield and Weight.

The following comparative statement, made up from official returns,
shows the average product per acre in various States of the Union, as
compared with the Canadian North-West, viz. :

Canadian North-West............26	Bush.	per.	acre.
Minnesota.....................17	"	"	"
Massachusetts.................16	"	"	"
Pennsylvania..................15	"	"	"
Wisconsin.....................13	"	"	"
Iowa.........................10	"	"	"
Ohio.........................10	"	"	"
Illinois...................... 8	"	"	"

These facts show the great superiority of the Canadian North West
as a wheat growing country. The weight of the wheat grown is also
something remarkable, especially when compared with that of other
countries. Taking the heaviest samples of each country we find :

Canadian North-West............66	lbs.	per	bush.
Minnesota.....................65	"	"	"
Ohio 60	"	"	"
Pennsylvania..................60	"	"	"
Illinois......................58	"	"	"

If more evidence is needed, it may be found in the speech made by
the Consul General of the United States for Manitoba, who, on the 3rd
October, 1879, made the following statement in regard to the flow of
emigration westward. He said that one of the great tides of emigration
now was to the Northern Zone, specially adapted to wheat growing
and cattle raising. That included Canada, Wisconsin, Michigan
partially. and Minnesota *but three-fourths of the great wheat producing belt of the continent lay north of the boundary. There the future
bread supply of America, and of the old world too, would be raised.*"
He went on to say " *that he wished to allude to that which was also of
very great moment, the meat supply. In his opinion the beef raised
in this northern district to which he had referred, would be found to
be superior in quality and superior in quantity to any that could be
raised even on the plains of Texas and the adjoining States.*"

The land requires no clearing of timber. It simply needs to be
ploughed, and in the same season produces excellent crops, thus
enabling settlers to avoid all the hardships known to backwoods-men
in clearing up heavily timbered lands.

Coarse Grains, Root Crops and Vegetables.

In addition to the great productiveness of the soil for wheat, it is
also admirably adapted for the growth of oats. barley and all other
kinds of grain, the yield per acre being very large. Roots and vegetables of all descriptions grow in the greatest profusion. The yield, as
exhibited at the agricultural shows throughout Canada, compares most
favourably with similar articles grown in other parts of the Dominion.

Oats

The oats grown in the Canadian North West are very superior i quality, being plump and heavy, and the yield per acre is simpl enormous, when compared with other countries As high as sevent bushels per acre is no uncommon thing, and in some cases even on hundred bushels have been realized.

For newly broken ground, oats will be found a most remunerativ crop, for which there is always a home market.

The comparison between the Canadian North-West and some of th American States as respects the yield of oats, is as follows .

Canadian North-West and some of the American States as respect the yield of oats, is as follows

Canadian North-West say average	57 bush. per acre		
Minnesota	"	37	"	"
Iowa	"	"	28	"	'
Ohio	"	"	23	'	"

Barley

Barley is grown very successfully as will be shown by the followin table The quality of the grain is excellent as a rule, its colour fin and brewers pronounce it second to none for malting purposes.

The following comparative statement tells its own tale

Canadian North-West say	40 bush. per acre.		
Minnesota.. ..	25	"	"	"
Iowa	22	"	"	"
Wisconsin	.20	"	"	"
Ohio ..	19	"	"	"
Indiana	19	"	"	"
Illinois	.17	"	"	"

Excellent beer is now being manufactured in Winnipeg from nativ barley.

Peas

Peas produce a very good crop and returns furnished to the Goveri ment, show the yield per acre to be in some instances as high as fror 60 to 68 bushels per acre, with an average weight per bushel of abou 60 lbs

Rye

Returns to Government show that the yield per acre averages fror 30 to 4, bushels, with an average weight of 60 lbs, per bushel Th crop has not hitherto been largely grown, but so far as known the yie has been very satisfactory.

Flax and Hemp.

The cultivation of Flax and Hemp during the early days of the Re River settlement was carried on successfully by the old settlers, but the same time the want of a market and the means to manufacture th raw material interfered with its profitable production then

Lately several of our farmers have paid some attention to the pr duction of these important crops, and the experience of those who hav tried them is certainly of a very satisfactory character. There is n the least doubt that as the climate of the North-West peculiarly fi ourable to the production of a good quality of both flax and hemp, the will play an important part in the future resources of the country flax mill has been constructed and is now in operation in Winnipeg.

Potatoes.

The Canadian North West is peculiarly adapted to the growth Potatoes The yield is enormous and the quality is well known to very superior. Some specimens weighed as high as $4\frac{3}{4}$ pounds eac and one peculiarity is that they are generally mealy to the very core The favourable climate and the rich soil of this country tend to ma

re very superior in
per acre is simply
As high as seventy
ome cases even one

most remunerative

est and some of the
follows
in States as respects

per acre.
"

"

wn by the following
rule, its colour fine
ng purposes.
n tale
sh. per acre.
  " "
  " "
  " "
  " "
  " "
  " "
Winnipeg from native

ished to the Govern-
nces as high as from
per bushel of about

er acre averages from
s, per bushel This
it as known the yield

arly days of the Red
ic old settlers, but at
is to manufacture the
ion then
attention to the pro-
ice of those who have
acter There is not
West peculiarly fav
h flax and hemp, they
s of the country A
ation in Winnipeg

ed to the growth of
is well known to be
as 4¾ pounds each,
ly to the very cor
country tend to make

---

the potato a profitable crop even during th
after breaking, by turning the sod over on

The average yield per acre as stated b
ranged from 300 to 320 bushels, and a nu
of 400 bushels of potatoes per acre   The
l as been from 55 to 60 lbs.

The following statements have been mad
actual experiences in Manitoba, and the No

W H J. Swain, of Morris,
    Has produced 800 to 1000 bushels of
      bushels of beans have also been raise

S C. Higginson, of Oakland.
    Has produced cabbages weighing 17½

Allan Bell, of Portage-La Prairie,
    Has had cabbages 45 inches around
    pounds each.

Beets.

A good deal of attention is already bein
Canada to the cultivation of the sugar bee
sugar, but there is no part of the Dominion
such paying quantities as in the North We
with which they can be cultivated, all tend
beet crops profitable, more especially when
beet, large quantities can be used for mana

Fruit Cultur

As yet the culture of fruit and apples in
fancy, but there is no doubt that certain va
fully   An abundance, however, of wild
berries, raspberries, whortleberries, cranbe
currants, blueberries and grapes, so that th
spect for the settler, and he will find the fla
North West most delicious   In Minnesot
was contended that apple trees would not
the Minnesota apple is a notable product o

Labor

There is a considerable demand for farm
part of the growing season, when good w
being about $20 per month with board.

In this way settlers, whose means are li
tide over the first season or two, by worki
neighbors, until such time as the increased
requires all their attention

"The most successful thin

The following statements made by actua
the authority of the Government, are th
proofs of the great advantages offered by M
West, as a most desireable field for immig

"I am a native of Western Ontario an
years. This is my fifth year here, and I
anywhere else   "JAMES Si

"I would just say that there are no obn
field is ready to be reaped, as a rule you c
Flax grows well in this country. I think
I have seen it grow as tall as I saw it in I

"Vegetables of all kinds grow splendid
with no manure.   "MATHEW OW

"I have been in the country six year
summer to give the best crops, even tho

the first season, immediately
on the seed.

by a number of farmers has
number have claimed a yield
he average weight per bushel

ade by farmers based on their
North West.

of turnips to the acre, and 60
used by him per acre.

1½ lbs. each.

nd, and turnips weighing 25

eing paid in different parts of
beet and its manufacture into
ion where it can be raised in
Vest. The rich soil, the ease
nd to make the production of
ien. as in the case of the sugar
nufacturing purposes.

ure.

n the North-West is in its in-
varities can be grown success-
d fruit exists, such as strawberries, plums, black and red
there is no scarcty in this re-
flavour of the wild fruit of the
sota, not many years ago. it
not grow there, and yet to-day
t of that State.

rm laborers during the greater
wages are paid, the average

limited, are often enabled to
rking as farm laborers for their
sed product of their own farms

hing is Success."

tual settlers and issued under
the best and most convincing
Manitoba and Canadian North
migration.
and have been farming fifteen
I much prefer this country to
STEWART, Meadow Lea."

hnoxious weeds here. When a
cannot see anything only grain
nk it can be grown with profit.
Ireland."
didly without much labor and
OWENS, J. P., High Bluff."
ars and have found the driest
hough there was no rain excep

the first season, immediately
>n the seed.
 by a number of farmers has
number have claimed a yield
1e average weight per bushel

ade by farmers based on their
North West.

of turnips to the acre, and 60
1ised by him per acre.

1½ lbs. each.

nd, and turnips weighing 25

eing paid in different parts of
>eet and its manufacture into
ion where it can be raised in
Vest. The rich soil, the ease
nd to make the production of
1en. as in the case of the sugar
nufacturing purposes.

ure.

n the North-West is in its in-
varities can be grown success-
d fruit exists, such as strawberries, plums, black and red
there is no scarc ty in this re-
flavour of the wild fruit of the
sota, not many years ago. it
1 >t grow there, and yet to-day
t of that State.

rm laborers during the greater
wages are paid, the average

: limited, are often enabled to
rking as farm laborers for their
sed product of their own farms

hing is Success.''

tual settlers and issued under
the best and most convincing
Manitoba and Canadian North
1igration.
an I have been farming fifteen
I I much prefer this country to
STEWART, Meadow Lea.''

bnoxious weeds here. When a
1 cannot see anything only grain
1k it can be grown with profit.
1 Ireland.''
didly without much labor and
JWENS, J. P., High Bluff.''
ars and have found t.............
hough there was no rain excep

an odd thunder-shower. New settlers should come in May and break their land till July, then after cutting and saving plenty of hay for all the cattle, they can prepare their buildings for the winter.
"HENRY WEST, Clear Springs."

"For stock-raising purposes the district is unequalled as the supply of hay is unlimited, and a man can raise as much stock as he is able to cut fodder for. "DAVID CHALMERS, St. Anne, Point Du Chêne."

"The potatoes raised here are the finest I ever saw. I have not been in the country but one year, but I am very well pleased with it. All kinds of roots grow better and larger here than in Ontario.
"WM. START, Assiniboine."

"I started with one cow, one horse and a plough 18 year ago, and to-day my assessement was for $13,000. I did not fail one crop yet in 18 years of my farming here, and I must say this year's crop is better than I have had before. You can depend upon me.
"BENJAMIN BRUCE, Poplar Point."

"Rye does well in this country. I have been in Scotland, England and the United States and in Ontario, but this country beats them all for large potatoes. "ROBERT BELL, Burnside."

"I would suggest that intending settlers in the North West who come to settle down on prairie land should break up an acre or two around where they build, on the West, North and East, and plant with maple seeds. Plant in rows four feet apart, the seeds to be planted one foot apart; they afterwards can be thinned out and transplanted. I have them 12 feet high, from the seed planted four years ago, and they will form a good shelter. I find, after a residence of nine years, that this North-West country is well calculated for raising the different kinds of grain sown by farmers. Market prices are very good. Wheat 85c. to $1 15, oats 50c. to 60c., and barley 60 cents.
"JAMES STEWART, High Bluff."

"Farmers should have Canadian horses, and get oxen and cows, and purchase young cattle. By so doing they will double their money every year. I am in the business and know by experience.
"JAMES McEWEN, Meadow Lea."

"There is no person need be afraid of this country for growing. There never was a better country under the Sun for either Hay or Grain." "A. V. BECKSTEAD, Emerson."

"Flax does extra well in this country."
"GEO. A. TUCKER, Portage-La Prairie."

"Native Hops here grow as large as any I ever saw cultivated."
"FRANCIS OGLETREE, Portage-La-Prairie."

"Hemp and Flax I have tried, and it grows excellently. Tame grasses of all kinds do well especialty Timothy. My advice to all is to come to this country, where they can raise the finest samples of grain of all kinds, that ever was raised in any country."
"ANDREW J. HINKER, Greenridge."

"Spring is the best time to come to this country as the settler can then get a crop of oats put in on breaking, which will yield him 25 bushels to the acre, and potatoes grow well ploughed under the sod. He can raise enough to keep him for the season. That way I raised 50 bushels from a quarter acre.
"ARTHUR D. CADENHEAD, Scratching River."

"Gentlemen,—The average yield of my grain last year, was: oats 65 bushels; wheat 30 bushels; potatoes 300 bushels; although some of my neighbours had over six hundred; turnips, I should say about 750 bushels, I would much rather take my chances here than to farm with the spade in any of the old countries. If you doubt my words please come and see for yourself." "JOHN BRYDON, Morris."

"Settlers should come without encumbering themselves with implements, etc., etc., as everything can be had at a cheap figure. Oxen we deem advisable to begin farming with.

"We expect to have a very plentiful though we sowed in May and June, April all is coming on well. Cucumbers growing had already. Melons and tomatoes we exp the end of this month or beginning of nex raspberries, and many other kinds of fruit are

"Bring your energy and capital with you hind you. Do not bring too much bagga after you arrive; they are quite as chea country. Be sure to locate a dry farm. Br season (June), when it ploughs easy and ro and potatoes. Barley don't do well on new l settlers. "ISAAC C

"I really think one cannot get a better I tell you, Sir, I have cropped 5 acres of lan successively without a rest, and this year a That is soil for you. I think immigrants country when they come here. You can't sa I wish them all good luck that come this brother farmers, come and help us plough u You can raise almost anything in this countr
"GEORGE TAYLOR, Popla

"I have run a threshing machine here for and the average of wheat is from 25 to 30 bus and barley 30 to 50. "JABEZ GEO.

"I have over 1,000 appletrees doing ver black currants. JAMES

"Having only had two years' experience to the country as I would like to do, for I country. I was nine years in Ontario, and and I prefer this country before either of ti everything. The three crops I have seen enab man that works in this country will like the something for his trouble. "EDW. J. JO

"Those who have no farms of their o Bring no horses; oxen are the things for a n
"JAMES

"Flax and hemp have been grown succ factured by hand, many years ago, both by old settlers. I have seen stalks of hemp gre
"JOHN SUTHERLAND,

"Let them come—this is the best countr with a few thousand dollars to go into stock. horses and have some eighty head of cattle, crops. I will have 60 to 70 bushels of oats
"JAMES FULLE

"From what I have seen in other countrie as any man can come to. For my part I hav could ever do in any other country. I rais have been men from California and other they said they never saw anything like it bef bushels to the acre of Black Sea wheat, and stood 6½ feet high, and not one straw of it glad if half of the people of Ireland were he be in the best part of the world. Every on well if it is not their own fault.
"JAMES OWENS, St. A

"Good advantages for settlers in this co pasturage. Can raise any quantity of stock v grain crop. Good water and plenty of woo
"JOHN HALL, St. A

e a very plentiful garden supply this year
ay and June, April being the usual time, yet
Cucumbers growing in the open air, we have
nd tomatoes we expect to have in any quantity
r beginning of next. Wild strawberries and
her kinds of fruit are to be had in abundance."
nd capital with you ; leave your prejudice be-
g too much baggage. Buy your implements
are quite as cheap and better suited to the
ate a dry farm. Break your land in the rainy
oughs easy and rots well. Sow wheat, oats
't do well on new land. Take advice from old
          "ISAAC CASSON, Greenbridge."

annot get a better farming country than this
pped 5 acres of land on my farm for six years
:st, and this year a better crop I never saw.
   think immigrants will be satisfied with this
here. You can't say too much in praise of it.
ck that come this way. All I say is come
d help us plough up this vast prairie country.
thing in this country.
RGE TAYLOR, Poplar Point, Long Lake."
ng machine here for the last five or six years,
is from 25 to 30 bushels, oats 40 to 60 bushels,
          "JABEZ GEO. BENT, Cook's Creek."
pletrees doing very well, and also excellent
          JAMES ARMSON, High Bluff.

'o years' experience here, I cannot do justice
ld like to do, for I believe it to be a good
.rs in Ontario, and in Ireland up to manhood,
   before either of them, taking the average of
ops I have seen enables me to believe that any
ountry will like the place, for he will have
.   "EDW. J. JOHNSTON, Springfield."

 farms of their own come here and farm.
re the things for a new settler.
          "JAMES AIRTH, Stonewall."
e been grown successfully here, and manu-
years ago, both by myself and several other
 stalks of hemp grow twelve feet high.
OHN SUTHERLAND, Senator, Kildonan."
 is the best country I ever struck for a man
rs to go into stock. I only raise oats for my
hty head of cattle, so cannot say much about
 70 bushels of oats to the acre this season.
          "JAMES FULLERTON, Cook's Creek."

:en in other countries this is as good a place
   For my part I have done better here than I
er country. I raised wheat here, and there
ifornia and other places, looking at it, and
anything like it before. One year I raised 35
ck Sea wheat, and I have raised wheat which
not one straw of it lay down. I would be
of Ireland were here, — and they would then
world. Every one who comes here can do
fault.
AMES OWENS, St. Anne, Pt.-Du-Chêne."

 settlers in this country ; plenty of hay and
 quantity of stock without interfering with the
and plenty of wood.
JOHN HALL, St. Anne, Pt.-Du-Chêne."

"We think this country cannot be beat for farming, and farmers can raise all the stock they want and cost them nothing, as they can cut all the hay on the prairie they want for winter feed, and their cattle will grow fat on it if well watered and cared for.
          "JAMES LAWRIE & BRO., Morris."

"Any man with $500, willing to work, can soon be independent here.   "ALEX. ADAMS, Clear Springs."

"I had twenty-eight acres in crop last year, and had eleven hundred bushels of grain, of which I sold four hundred and fifty dollars' worth, besides having feed for my team and bread for my family.
          "JAMES DAVIDSON, High Bluff."

The following experience of Mr. H. M. Power will convey some idea of what can be accomplished in farming on a large scale, in the Canadian North West.

"Mr. H. M. Power came from Herefordshire England to this country, early in 1882. After inspecting various parts of the country he finally decided to purchase five and a half sections, containing 3,520 acres from the C. P. R., on their then price with their rebate allowance for settlement. He entered upon the land in June, 1882, and broke some land that year. It is situated between Virden and Fort Ellice about 200 miles West of Winnipeg. In 1883 he broke a large quantity. He began putting stock upon the farm in the fall of 1882. I will now describe what I found to be the condition of affairs after but little more than two years of work. I found 1,240 acre of wheat, in first rate condition, with a probable average yield of 25 bushels to the acre : 40 acres of barley, and 260 acres of oats. I drove round all the fields, and a finer growth of cereals it would be hard to find. The poorest crop is the oats, which appears to be the case wherever I have been. Potatoes, turnips, and other vegetables were all excellent crops. The wheat is beginning to turn yellow at the bottom, and it is expected that in about a fortnight harvesting will commence, and that by the end of August nearly, if not quite, the whole crop will be safely gathered. All the land now under crop was plowed last fall. Seeding was begun on the 2nd of April, and the wheat was all sown by the first week in May. Two hundred and sixty acres in addition have been broken this year. They are now cutting and putting up 500 tons of hay for the use of the cattle next winter. There are nine houses and four barns now on the farm for the workmen, horses, etc., and it is intended to erect three or four more. There are now 203 head of cattle on the farm feeding in the valley of the Assiniboine, where there is magnificent pasturage, ample water, and shelter in the wood on the slopes. Seventy-six calves have been born during the last two years, and beginning with next year there will be a good supply of three year old steers to the butchers. The cattle look remarkably well and the calves of this year, as also the yearlings and two-year-olds, are all large and strong. At each house broods of chickens are being raised. At present there are 38 pigs, sows and litters, which it is expected will increase to 100 at least by the fall.

"This is not a very bad record of growth in two years. But it is not all. Mr. Power has a section of 640 acres near Moosomin, on which there are 125 acres with a fine crop of wheat, and 75 acres broken this year to put under crop next year. At the two farms on the Assiniboine, and at Moosomin, there will be a probable yield of about 34,000 bushels of wheat, which, deducting 6,000 bushels for seed for next year, will leave a probable quantity for sale of from 20,000 to 28,000 bushels, according as the yield actually turns out. Mr. Power also purchased seven sections, or nearly 5,000 acres, at Whitewood, where he has this year broken 1,000 acres to put under crop next year. He will thus have at the three places about 3,000 acres of land to put under crop next year. His land is all broken and backset before being sown, and is plowed in the fall, so as to be sown

e a very plentiful garden supply this year
ay and June, April being the usual time, yet
Cucumbers growing in the open air, we have
nd tomatoes we expect to have in any quantity
r beginning of next. Wild strawberries and
her kinds of fruit are to be had in abundance."
nd capital with you ; leave your prejudice be-
g too much baggage. Buy your implements
are quite as cheap and better suited to the
ate a dry farm. Break your land in the rainy
oughs easy and rots well. Sow wheat, oats
't do well on new land. Take advice from old
    "ISAAC CASSON, Greenbridge."

annot get a better farming country than this
opped 5 acres of land on my farm for six years
st, and this year a better crop I never saw.

think immigrants will be satisfied with this
here. You can't say too much in praise of it.
ck that come this way. All I say is come
d help us plough up this vast prairie country.
thing in this country.
RGE TAYLOR, Poplar Point, Long Lake."

ng machine here for the last five or six years,
is from 25 to 30 bushels, oats 40 to 60 bushels,
    "JABEZ GEO. BENT, Cook's Creek."
ppletrees doing very well, and also excellent
    JAMES ARMSON, High Bluff."

'o years' experience here, I cannot do justice
ld like to do, for I believe it to be a good
.rs in Ontario, and in Ireland up to manhood,
before either of them, taking the average of
ops I have seen enables me to believe that any
ountry will like the place, for he will have
.   "EDW. J. JOHNSTON, Springfield."

farms of their own come here and farm.
re the things for a new settler.
    "JAMES AIRTH, Stonewall."
e been grown successfully here, and manu-
years ago, both by myself and several other
stalks of hemp grow twelve feet high.
OHN SUTHERLAND, Senator, Kildonan."
it the best country I ever struck for a man
rs to go into stock. I only raise oats for my
hty head of cattle, so cannot say much about
70 bushels of oats to the acre this season.
    "JAMES FULLERTON, Cook's Creek."

en in other countries this is as good a place
For my part I have done better here than I
er country. I raised wheat here, and there
fornia and other places, looking at it, and
anything like it before. One year I raised 35
ck Sea wheat, and I have raised wheat which
not one straw of it lay down. I would be
of Ireland were here, – and they would then
world. Every one who comes here can do
fault.
AMES OWENS, St. Anne, Pt.-Du-Chêne."
settlers in this country ; plenty of hay and
quantity of stock without interfering with the
and plenty of wood.
JOHN HALL, St. Anne, Pt.-Du-Chêne."

"We think this country cannot be beat for farming, and farmers can raise all the stock they want and cost them nothing, as they can cut all the hay on the prairie they want for winter feed, and their cattle will grow fat on it if well watered and cared for.
    "JAMES LAWRIE & BRO , Morris."

"Any man with $500, willing to work, can soon be independent here.   "ALEX. ADAMS, Clear Springs."

"I had twenty-eight acres in crop last year, and had eleven hundred bushels of grain, of which I sold four hundred and fifty dollars' worth, besides having feed for my team and bread for my family.
    "JAMES DAVIDSON, High Bluff."

The following experience of Mr. H. M. Power will convey some idea of what can be accomplished in farming on a large scale, in the Canadian North West.

"Mr. H. M. Power came from Herefordshire England to this country, early in 1882. After inspecting various parts of the country he finally decided to purchase five and a half sections, containing 3,520 acres from the C. P. R., on their then price with their rebate allowance for settlement. He entered upon the land in June, 1882, and broke some land that year. It is situated between Virden and Fort Ellice about 200 miles West of Winnipeg. In 1883 he broke a large quantity. He began putting stock upon the farm in the fall of 1882. I will now describe what I found to be the condition of affairs after but little more than two years of work. I found 1,240 acre of wheat, in first rate condition, with a probable average yield of 25 bushels to the acre ; 40 acres of barley, and 260 acres of oats. I drove round all the fields, and a finer growth of cereals it would be hard to find. The poorest crop is the oats, which appears to be the case wherever I have been. Potatoes, turnips, and other vegetables were all excellent crops. The wheat is beginning to turn yellow at the bottom, and it is expected that in about a fortnight harvesting will commence, and that by the end of August nearly, if not quite, the whole crop will be safely gathered. All the land now under crop was plowed last fall. Seeding was begun on the 2nd of April, and the wheat was all sown by the first week in May. Two hundred and sixty acres in addition have been broken this year. They are now cutting and putting up 500 tons of hay for the use of the cattle next winter. There are nine houses and four barns now on the farm for the workmen, horses, etc., and it is intended to erect three or four more. There are now 203 head of cattle on the farm feeding in the valley of the Assiniboine, where there is magnificent pasturage, ample water, and shelter in the wood on the slopes. Seventy-six calves have been born during the last two years, and beginning with next year there will be a good supply of three year old steers to the butchers. The cattle look remarkably well and the calves of this year, as also the yearlings and two-year-olds, are all large and strong. At each house broods of chickens are being raised. At present there are 38 pigs, sows and litters, which it is expected will increase to 100 at least by the fall.

"This is not a very bad record of growth in two years. But it is not all. Mr. Power has a section of 640 acres near Moosomin, on which there are 125 acres with a fine crop of wheat, and 75 acres broken this year to put under crop next year. At the two farms on the Assiniboine, and at Moosomin, there will be a probable yield of about 34,000 bushels of wheat, which, deducting 6,000 bushels for seed for next year, will leave a probable quantity for sale of from 20,000 to 28,000 bushels, according as the yield actually turns out. Mr. Power also purchased seven sections, or nearly 5,000 acres, at Whitewood, where he has this year broken 1,000 acres to put under crop next year. He will thus have at the three places about 3,000 acres of land to put under crop next year. His land is all broken and backset before being sown, and is plowed in the fall, so as to be sown

an odd thunder-shower. New settlers should come in May and break their land till July, then after cutting and saving plenty of hay for all the cattle, they can prepare their buildings for the winter.

"HENRY WEST, Clear Springs."

"For stock-raising purposes the district is unequalled as the supply of hay is unlimited, and a man can raise as much stock as he is able to cut fodder for. "DAVID CHALMERS, St. Anne, Point Du Chêne."

"The potatoes raised here are the finest I ever saw. I have not been in the country but one year, but I am very well pleased with it. All kinds of roots grow better and larger here than in Ontario.

"WM. START, Assiniboine "

"I started with one cow, one horse and a plough 18 year ago, and to-day my assessment was for $13,000. I did not fail one crop yet in 18 years of my farming here, and I must say this year's crop is better than I have had before. You can depend upon me.

"BENJAMIN BRUCE, Poplar Point."

"Rye does well in this country. I have been in Scotland, England and the United States and in Ontario, but this country beats them all for large potatoes. "ROBERT BELL, Burnside "

"I would suggest that intending settlers in the North West who come to settle down on prairie land should break up an acre or two around where they build, on the West, North and East, and plant with maple seeds Plant in rows four feet apart, the seeds to be planted one foot apart; they afterwards can be thinned out and transplanted. I have them 12 feet high, from the seed planted four years ago, and they will form a good shelter. I find, after a residence of nine years, that this North-West country is well calculated for raising the different kinds of grain sown by farmers Market prices are very good. Wheat 85c. to $1 15, oats 50c. to 60c, and barley 60 cents.

"JAMES STEWART, High Bluff."

"Farmers should have Canadian horses, and get oxen and cows, and purchase young cattle. By so doing they will double their money every year. I am in the business and know by experience.

"JAMES McEWEN, Meadow Lea."

"There is no person need be afraid of this country for growing. There never was a better country under the Sun for either Hay or Grain." "A. V. BECKSTEAD, Emerson."

"Flax does extra well in this country.

"GEO. A. TUCKER, Portage-La-Prairie."

"Native Hops here grow as large as any I ever saw cultivated."

"FRANCIS OGLETREE, Portage-La-Prairie."

"Hemp and Flax I have tried, and it grows excellently. Tame grasses of all kinds do well especialty Timothy. My advice to all is to come to this country, where they can raise the finest samples of grain of all kinds, that ever was raised in any country."

"ANDREW J. HINKER, Greenridge."

"Spring is the best time to come to this country as the settler can then get a crop of oats put in on breaking, which will yield him 25 bushels to the acre, and potatoes grow well ploughed under the sod. He can raise enough to keep him for the season. That way I raised 50 bushels from a quarter acre.

"ARTHUR D. CADENHEAD, Scratching River."

"Gentlemen,—The average yield of my grain last year, was: oats 65 bushels; wheat 30 bushels; potatoes 300 bushels; although some of my neighbours had over six hundred; turnips, I should say about 750 bushels, I would much rather take my chances here than to farm with the spade in any of the old countries. If you doubt my words please come and see for yourself." "JOHN BRYDON, Morris."

"Settlers should come without encumbering themselves with implements, etc., etc. as everything can be had at a cheap figure. Oxen we deem advisable to begin farming with.

"We expect to have a very plentifu
though we sowed in May and June, April
all is coming on well. Cucumbers growing
had already. Melons and tomatoes we exp
the end of this month or beginning of nex
raspberries, and many other kinds of fruit are

"Bring your energy and capital with you
hind you. Do not bring too much bagga
after you arrive; they are quite as chea
country. Be sure to locate a dry farm. Br
season (June), when it ploughs easy and ro
and potatoes. Barley don't do well on new l
settlers. "ISAAC C

"I really think one cannot get a better
I tell you. Sir, I have cropped 5 acres of lan
successively without a rest, and this year a
That is soil for you. I think immigrants
country when they come here. You can't sa
I wish them all good luck that come this
brother farmers, come and help us plough u
You can raise almost anything in this countr
"GEORGE TAYLOR, Popla

"I have run a threshing machine here fo
and the average of wheat is from 25 to 30 bus
and barley 30 to 50. "JABEZ GEO,

"I have over 1,000 appletrees doing ver
black currants. JAMES

"Having only had two years' experience
to the country as I would like to do, for I
country. I was nine years in Ontario, and
and I prefer this country before either of th
everything. The three crops I have seen enab
man that works in this country will like the
something for his trouble. "EDW. J. JOI

"Those who have no farms of their o
Bring no horses; oxen are the things for a n
"JAMES

"Flax and hemp have been grown succ
factured by hand, many years ago, both by
old settlers. I have seen stalks of hemp gr
"JOHN SUTHERLAND,

"Let them come—this is the best countr
with a few thousand dollars to go into stock.
horses and have some eighty head of cattle,
crops. I will have 60 to 70 bushels of oats
"JAMES FULLE

"From what I have seen in other countrie
as any man can come to For my part I hav
could ever do in any other country. I rais
have been men from California and other
they said they never saw anything like it bef
bushels to the acre of Black Sea wheat, and
stood 6½ feet high, and not one straw of it
glad if half of the people of Ireland were he
be in the best part of the world. Every on
well if it is not their own fault.

"JAMES OWENS, St. A

"Good advantages for settlers in this co
pasturage. Can raise any quantity of stock v
grain crop. Good water and plenty of woo
"JOHN HALL, St. A

as early as possible in the spring. On these three farms there are 12 horses, 18 working oxen and 29 mules

"Other similar cases, although not on so large a scale, could readily be brought forward. At Virden, close to the station, Messrs Bouverie and Rutledge started in this year and have broken 550 acres, which they will backset this fall, and sow with wheat next spring They have also started a small herd of cattle Within sight of the station, close to where I camped three years ago, Mr. W. Stephen has built a comfortable house and barn, picturesquely placed in a grove of trees on the bank of Gopher creek He has already broken a good deal of ground, and has a fine herd of about 100 head of cattle. South, in the direction of Pipe-tone creek, the land is thickly settled, and on every side are to do seen large fields of waving wheat, just beginning to turn under the powerful rays of the sun, and a large extent of newly broken ground to be put under crop next year

"It is estimated that at Virden there will be about 200,000 bushels of wheat to sell this year, and at Elkhorn about 75 000 bushels. It is very earnestly to be hoped that there will be sufficient buyers come forward to deal with such quantities as these, supplemented by what will pour in for sale at other stations, and thus avoid a recurrence of last year's operations, which, by a practical monopoly, heavily reduced the price paid to the farmers.

"The facts stated are all important and encouraging"

Cattle Raising

The country is well adapted for raising cattle, the prairie grass being peculiarly nourishing and exists in large quantities It also makes excellent hay, the only expense being the cost of cutting and drawing to the farm yard. So excellent is the prairie grass that cattle driven for hundreds of miles across the plains, show no falling off in weight and condition as they proceed on their journey The abundance of grass and hay, and the excellent root crops which are grown, render the raising of large herds of cattle extremely profitable

Horses remain out during the winter, the depth of snow being light, and when brought in in spring, are not in much worse condition than when turned out at the beginning of winter.

Absence of Disease

One of the strongest points in favor of this country as a field for cattle raising is the entire absence of those diseases which have played such havoc amongst the herds on the plains of Texas and in Montana, and which has had the effect of excluding them entirely from European markets

Sheep Raising.

The same advantages in connection with the raising of the larger class of stock apply also to sheep, and the experience of many of our old settlers shows conclusively that wool growing in the Canadian North West is a branch of industry which will prove of great profit to every farmer engaging in it

Poultry.

The raising of poultry is now almost universal throughout Manitoba, and has been attended with the greatest possible success. The cost of keeping poultry is exceedingly small, and, in proportion, the profits are large.

Pigs.

The raising of pigs is now being gone into extensively, and wherever it has been tried, it has proved a successful venture Pigs thrive very satisfactorily in this country, and their keeping is attended with but little trouble and expense.

Pork packing establishments have already been started in Winnipeg

Climate

The climate of Manitoba and the North-W Fever and ague, which exist in so many par are here unknown In summer the heat is and though amply sufficient for the thorough no greater than in Ontario, or throughout t of the continent. In winter the cold is ste rule, than is met with in all parts of the we nent north of Chicago The fall of snow is of Canada, seldom reaching two feet in d climate is an excellent one, both as regards tants and the maturing of the crops

The story of summer frosts has long since in this respect there are occasional exceptio but any farmer can make himself perfectly s care to sow his seed as early as possible in t

The dryness of the air to a great degree frosts, of a nature to injure crops

The Canadian North-West is specially storms and while we hear of hurricanes de other portions of the American continent, so known north of the 49th parallel of latitude

There has not been a case of crops having in this country for many years, and in winter snow storm so frequently experienced to the

The country is certainly blessed in this respe sometimes intense, the weather is generally c

Another blessing so far enjoyed by the far territory of Canada is the freedom from bligh in other parts of the continent have been so

The following statements, by actual sett of the climate on cattle proves conclusively ary, for successfully raising stock exist in Canadian North West, than any where else

Benj Hartley	St. Charles	Animals do n England
A Gillespie.	Greenwood .	Animals do
S C Higginson	Oakland	The winter suffer from
J Sutherland	Kildonan, E	The winter in more so
Adam Bell	Portage-La-Prairie	Animals tur
James Sturton	Nelsonville	Climate bein better th u
John Ferguson	High Bluff	Cattle are as the clin
D W. Johnston	Springfield	The winter
Bullantyne	West Lynne	Although la cold, cattle
John Biggs .	Morris	I have know the straw
Angus Polson	Kildonan	The winter native pon
Thos Sigsons	Portage-La-Prairie	The winters favorable well
Thos Dalzell	High Bluff	The winter as in Onta to freeze o
W. A Mann	Bird's Hill.	Cattle do bet ter than n
John Fraser	Kildonan .	The winter, therefore
W A Farmer	Headingly .	The winter are remark
H C Graham	Stonewall ...	The dryness the cold
James Stewart	High Bluff . ..	Stock will b Ontario an

Climate.

a and the North-West is exceedingly healthy.
...ist in so many parts of the Western States,
ummer the heat is by no means oppressive,
nt for the thorough maturity of the crops, is
o, or throughout the North-Western portion
ater the cold is steady, and no greater, as a
all parts of the western portion of the conti-
The fall of snow is lighter than in most parts
hing two feet in depth. On the whole, the
e, both as regards the health of the inhabi-
the crops.
osts has long since been exploded. Of course,
ccasional exceptions, as in other countries,
himself perfectly secure from loss, by taking
rly as possible in the spring.
to a great degree tends to prevent summer
re crops.
West is specially favored in freedom from
r of hurricanes devastating whole districts in
erican continent, such things are almost un-
parallel of latitude.
ase of crops having been destroyed by storms
years, and in winter we do not have the severe
y experienced to the south of us
blessed in this respect, and although the cold is
ather is generally calm and clear when it is so.
enjoyed by the farmers of the North Western
freedom from blight, worms or insects, which
nent have been so destructive to crops.
nts, by actual settlers in regard to the effect
roves conclusively that the conditions necess-
sing stock exist in a greater degree in the
an any where else :—

....	Animals do not suffer so much here as in England.
....	Animals do well here in winter.
....	The winters are dry ; animals do not suffer from cold.
E..	The winter is less severe on animals than in more southern latitudes.
Prairie	Animals turn out well in the spring.
....	Climate being dryer, animals stand cold better than in Ontario
....	If cattle are well cared for, they thrive, as the climate is dry.
....	The winter is not severer than in Ontario.
c..	Although last winter was exceptionally cold, cattle wintered well.
....	I have known young cattle to winter at the straw pile.
....	The winter is not severe on animals ; native ponies winter out.
Prairie	The winters being dry and frosty, they are favorable to cattle ; they eat their food well.
...	The winter is not so hard on cattle here as in Ontario, as there is no rain or sleet to freeze on them.
....	Cattle do better here in a cold steady winter than a changeable one.
....	The winter, though cold, is uniform, and therefore not unfavourable to animals.
....	The winter is not severe on animals ; they are remarkably healthy.
....	The dryness of the atmosphere neutralizes the cold.
....	Stock will be as fat in the spring as in Ontario and Quebec.

D. Chalmers....	St. Anne Pt. D. C.	The winter is less severe on animals here than in Ontario.
Matthew Ferris	Burnside......	The winter not much severer here on animals than in Ontario.
J. W. Carelton	Clear Springs.....	Animals thrive well in the cold season.
M. Owens......	High Bluff........	The winters here are less severe on cattle than in Ontario
Nelson Brown..	High Bluff........	The winters here have about the same effects on animals as in Ontario.
J. McKinnon...	Portage-La-Prairie	Cattle thrive well in winter if properly fed.
James Stewart	Meadow Lea......	Young cattle grow all the winter when warmly stabled and fed on wild hay.

It may also be interesting for intending settlers to known how the farmers of the North-West winter their cattle, and for this reason, we give a few instances :

TESTIMONY OF SETTLERS RESPECTING WINTERING OF CATTLE.

W. Jackson...	High Bluff...	I stable my cattle at night and let them run in the yard during the day.
S. C. Higginson	Oakland...........	I winter my cattle in much the same way as in Ontario.
Jno. Ferguson	High Bluff........	I house my cattle and feed them on hay and they are in good condition in the spring.
Robt. Fisher...	Cook's Creek......	I house the cattle warmly and feed them on hay with an occasional feed of salt.
A. J. Moore....	Nelsonville	I feed the cattle on wild hay and turn the steers and young stock loose in the straw stacks.
Jno. Geddis....	Kildonan........	Cows are kept in the stable and other cattle fed in the yard on hay and straw and stabled at night.
A. McDonald..	Gladstone....	I stable cows and working cattle and the young stock run loose around the straw stcks.
A. P. Stevenson	Nelsonville.......	The cows are stabled and the young cattle run out all the winter.
F. Ogletree....	Portage-La-Prairie	I stable my cows and allow my young cattle to run around the straw stacks.
G. Granby....	High Bluff........	I feed my cattle on wild hay and turn them out to the straw stacks in the day time.
And. Nelson...	Stonewall....	I stable my cattle and feed them on prairie hay.
Wm. Hill......	Woodlands.......	I stable my cattle, my native ponies are out.
Robt. Bell.....	Rockwood.	I stable my cattle in a flat roof log building with straw on the top.
Jno. George....	Nelsonville	I feed my cattle on hay, turnips or grain are required if straw is used.
A. McPherson..	Emerson	I keep my cattle stabled, from December to the end of March.
Robt. Bell......	Burnside..........	We stable our cows and oxen and let the young cattle run out in sheds.
Robt. Morgan..	Headingly.........	I keep my cattle in stables during the winter.
Matthew Ferris	Burnside..........	I keep the cows and calves in stables, the rest run around the straw stacks most of the winter.
J. W. Carleton	Clear Springs.....	I keep my cattle in warm stables, giving them plenty of hay and water.
Nelson Brown..	High Bluff........	I feed my cattle in a yard on native hay and stable them.

Steamers on Saskatchewan River.

A line of steamers runs up the Saskatchewan River from Grand Rapids at the mouth of the river to Prince Albert, Carlton, Battleford, Fort Pitt, and on to Edmonton at the base of the Rocky Mountains These steamers connect with a line of first class steamers running between Winnipeg and Grand Rapids.

During the past two years a considerable sum of money has been expended by the Dominion Government in removing obstructions to the navigation of the North Saskatchewan river and generally improv-

CPSIA information can be obtained at www.ICGtesting.com
Printed in the USA
LVOW03s2224120214

373411LV00020B/1024/P